WHAT PEOPLE ARE SAYING ABOUT

SEE*ING

"I have known Keith I   Ve live on
opposite sides of the p   nuch, but
every time we get toge   ...ies about our journey
towards a wholehearted love that seeks hard after justice. In
Seeking Justice Keith gets to share his journey in the depth and the
detail that we could never have in a single conversation. In
Seeking Justice Keith helps us see the world through the eyes of a
radical compassion that embraces beauty, rebels against brutality
and commits itself resolutely to work slowly but surely to create
a better future, In *Seeking Justice* Keith shares the way to engage
in change with great care, so we can envisage what it would
mean for us to do likewise."
Dave Andrews, well known speaker, activist, author, and
member of the Waiters Union, Brisbane

"This book is as exciting as it is important - both profoundly
spiritual and intensely practical, passionately calling us to seek
and work for justice within our neighbourhood and all creation.
With a single sweep Keith strips away the seemingly benign
camouflage clothing our society to reveal its monstrous reality,
then shows us how - with God's strength - we can be part of
building the new world within the shell of the old. *Seeking Justice*
is unashamedly Jesus focused, but draws wisdom from many
faiths and beliefs. Filled with personal stories of activism that
blaspheme the gods and powers of the status quo, it gives us the
tools we need. This book inspires a creative imagination that is
visceral and tactile in its peace building, without any hint of
violence but saturated in the radical compassion of true love. If
you long for change *Seeking Justice* is for you."
Noel Moules is a thinker, teacher and activist for peace, justice

and deep ecology. He is creator and director of the Workshop programme for applied spirituality and a founder member of the Anabaptist Network UK. He is the author of, *Fingerprints of Fire ... Footprints of Peace*.

"It is a dangerous book that dares to build a thesis on Jesus' allusion to 'binding the strong man' in Mark 3:27. It is about time that we in Britain had access to a 'home grown' dangerous book that makes the most of insights from American writers who have spotlighted the radical nature of Jesus' performance. The countless examples and stories of resistance and action rooted in neighborhoods up and down Britain make for a story line that would grace many pages of the Sunday supplements – and no doubt cause consternation. Keith Hebden makes visible what has been happening 'underground' over the last decade. This book is an implicit celebration of what happens when we are able to read the Gospels in their fullness, not constrained by lectionaries and other limiters. Ian Frazer, now of the Iona Community, wrote a wonderful book, *Reinventing Theology as the People's Work*; when he wrote it in 1980 it seemed aspirational. The book that you now have in your hand suggests that the radicalness of the Gospels cannot remain domesticated when those who are being marginalized are able to learn from Jesus of Nazareth. The Gospels are dangerous and so is this book because it is now impossible to be content with institution-serving efforts at mission."

Ann Morisy is a community theologian and the author of the best-selling books *Beyond the Good Samaritan* and *Journeying Out*. She lectures widely and leads workshops, both in the UK and abroad.

Seeking Justice

The Radical Compassion of Jesus

Seeking Justice

The Radical Compassion of Jesus

Revd Dr Keith Hebden

Winchester, UK
Washington, USA

First published by Circle Books, 2013

Circle Books is an imprint of John Hunt Publishing Ltd., Laurel House, Station Approach, Alresford, Hants, SO24 9JH, UK
office1@jhpbooks.net
www.johnhuntpublishing.com
www.circle-books.com

For distributor details and how to order please visit the 'Ordering' section on our website.

Text copyright: Keith Hebden 2012

ISBN: 978 1 78099 688 2

A CIP catalogue record for this book is available from the British Library.

Design: Stuart Davies

Printed and bound by CPI Group (UK) Ltd, Croydon, CR0 4YY

We operate a distinctive and ethical publishing philosophy in all areas of our business, from our global network of authors to production and worldwide distribution.

CONTENTS

Foreword

The long-term pursuit of compassionate activists is the skilling-up of individuals and communities in personal and social healing stories and techniques.
Keith Hebden

When Walter Wink died in 2012, the world lost an important example of 'compassionate activism'. He had dedicated himself to struggles of nonviolence, and to communicating those struggles to the world through thoughtful and active academia. Wink's trilogy *Naming the Powers*, *Unmasking the Powers* and *Engaging the Powers* gave activists a manual to help reflect on the world as it really is, whilst giving us the tools with which to begin to tackle the issues surrounding us. Militarism, racism, and corporate power begin to make sense when we examine the notion of 'powers and principalities' and how they manifest themselves in the here and now.

This book is a profound continuation of Wink's work, both theoretically and practically. Keith Hebden brings an incisive mind to the real-life dilemmas of modern capitalism, and offers helpful analysis. Significantly, he begins to map a faithful response to the violence and horror of our society.

The reason why this book is so important is that the author is committing himself to these struggles as an obvious part of his mission and ministry. His knowledge is based not just on his reading, but on painful experience. He is prepared to stand up and challenge violence from the pulpit, even if it means being thrown out of a cathedral. He will place his body on the road to blockade Aldermaston, the place in the UK where the mad logic of nuclear weapons technology begins. He will risk abuse by those with power when he challenges the impact of austerity politics on his local community.

The real joy of this book is that it so effortlessly translates this activity and passion into such an articulate piece of theological reasoning. Theology begins to make sense. For so many, theology taught in academia has borne little relation to the experiences of the men and women we encounter in life outside our training institutions. It rarely touched on the bigger issues of consumerism, sexism, racism, economic inequality and ecological suicide. Yet these are the issues of our day, and our theology must not only make sense of it, but must be part of the mechanism of transforming it.

One of Hebden's key ideas is the transformation of the dehumanizing term 'individualism' into the community-building properties of 'personalism'. Individualism is the cornerstone of some of the most corrosive elements of the neo-liberal agenda that we face in the 21st century. It forces us to constantly compare ourselves to others; to promote our needs over the needs of others. It leads to accumulation, competition, rivalry, and ultimately internalizes violence and the dehumanization of the 'other'. Personalism is the exact opposite: it involves a process of relationship with each human encounter that leads to sharing, peacemaking and a desire to meet God in the other. Personalism leads to communal activities and mutual aid which can transform society towards the common good. In this analysis, we see a development within Christian anarchism that is profoundly useful to our ways of understanding ourselves and our society.

For those of us who still have an interest in the Bible, there is much on offer in this book. The concept of the good shepherd is well defined here. It loses the traditional misguided paternalistic interpretations and instead becomes a tool for radical community organizing. All of us need to become good shepherds, opening our doors to the marginalized and forgotten. The ecological insight gained from the commentary on Luke chapter 15 (the prodigal son) is astounding and will stay with readers for a lifetime. One of the most helpful observations is in the analysis of the turning of the tables in the temple. In this deliberate attack on the systems of domination in Jerusalem, Jesus cannot possibly have acted alone, and must have involved the community of disciples for it to have been successful. This interpretation helps us understand Jesus as a community activist enabling others to be part of the transformative process, not just someone acting as a maverick leader. Through Jesus, God seeks to build up communities of resistance, love and justice, and that can only begin when people are participants in their liberation, and not just bystanders. This book constantly looks at ways in which to shock our perceptions so that hidden realities can be exposed. It makes helpful connections between our Bibles and our actions. That is, after all, the only way it can ever be good news in the truest sense.

This book is at its best when describing how practical resistance to the powers of domination actually works. The chapter on prophecy, lament, meek refusal, direct action and subversion will be instructive for anyone who wants to seriously challenge the way society is currently organized for the benefit of the few. For those of us inspired by groups such as Christian Peacemaker Teams and the 'Occupy movement', we must understand the underlying philosophy that underpins challenges to the status quo. Only then will we withstand the inevitable institutional attacks on these movements in general and our own actions in particular. The final chapter on 'principles of compassionate resistance' is a systematic guide in helping us use the teachings of Jesus, Gandhi and Dorothy Day in our everyday resistance to oppression. In daring to 'create the future', 'love the other' and engage with other such principles, we learn about our true selves, and begin to trust that it is possible to resist the evils of this world. This is an important discovery in a society that constantly frowns on activism. We can easily succumb to systems of fear and submission if we have not fully understood the grave nature of the situation, and have not looked deep into our own personal reserves to face up to the 'powers'.

This is an optimistic book: 'Public, radical compassion is as joyful as it is costly.' We discover the wonders of humanity when we learn to build better societies and challenge existing ones. We discover God fully at work, and faith and hope is strengthened. This book is part of a growing sea-change in British theology that is asking serious questions about the nature of the Church and the nature of our faith. It demands that we make sense of the 'powers that be', and that we become wary of how they dominate our institutions and infiltrate even our own psychological under-standing of the world. The monsters need taming, and the messengers need tripping up.

I hope when you have fully digested this book, you will seek out some of the organizations referenced within it, and join with them. Better still, you will have the skills and the confidence to build local alliances right in your own community. After all, there is no better place to begin bringing about the reign of God's compassion.

Chris Howson

Chris Howson is currently working as a chaplain in Sunderland, having spent ten years ministering in Bradford city center. He is a popular speaker and community activist and his first book is entitled *A Just Church: 21st Century Liberation Theology in Action*.

Preface

This book is intended as a lab book for your experiments in social transformation, alongside others who care about the same issues you care about. It is a tool box of principles, strategies, and ways of rethinking reality that you're invited to take part in. So I encourage you to read this book with other people. If you use the website, or the group work ideas at the end of each chapter, share with others what does and doesn't work. You are invited to become part of the story of this book by critiquing and testing what you find here. I look forward to hearing from you and learning from your experiments in truth.

Because I wrote this book out of the experience of working with others and listening to their stories, I could fill several pages with the names of people who made it possible, or rather, who need to take some responsibility for the end result.

Many of the ideas and experiences grew out of time spent at places like All Hallows in Leeds, The Queen's Foundation in Birmingham, SoulSpace in Bradford, and the London Catholic Workers. These communities have been a constant source of inspiration and encouragement. But I also owe much to the anarchist movement in London and Simon Barrow and Jonathan Bartley who set up the incredible think-tank Ekklesia. Anyone who has been involved in one of my workshops knows I owe them a lot for criticizing, adapting and extending many of the ideas you will find in here.

I also want to give particular thanks to John M. Hull at The Queen's Foundation for the adventures we went on together and for believing in me while we set about causing the right kind of trouble, and Al and Janey for their friendship and inspiration. All the readers and contributors to A Pinch of Salt and Jesus Radicals have helped me think through these ideas and my own practice.

This book was written while I was training as an Anglican

priest in Gloucester diocese. Many clergy and staff in the diocese have encouraged and valued my particular way of 'being a priest', showing patience and openness. Hugh Dickinson as 'spiritual accompanier' and proofreader of this book has helped me along the way. Most of all, the congregations and community of Matson have given me the space to experiment, think, and write stuff down. Jeni Parsons, who supervised my training as priest, has been a constant challenge and source of humor and friendship, and gave me some important feedback on the first draft of this book; most of which I haven't ignored. The community and I have much to be thankful for in her priestly ministry in Matson.

Most of all I need to thank Sophie, whom I'm blessed to have as my companion for life. She is wise to my excesses, invites me to play more, and tempers with compassion my often-dogmatic approach to life. I can't think of anyone I admire more than her.

On Machismo

Just before this book was published I wrote to community theologian Ann Morisy. This was part of her reply: '... as long as you finger masculinity as a bugbear ... I'm getting tired of radical thinkers who fail to see the disruption to the creation associated with unreflected and uncontrolled "will to power"!' *Oh, crap!* I thought; *I don't know if I did?* While writing this book I discovered that almost all my named influences, especially writers, are men. I wondered if there just weren't many women writing radical Christian stuff so I had a look around and discovered I was just sharing a widely held prejudice: just one of several personal prejudices I discovered in the writing task. Ann Morisy is right, of course: there is much in the activist world that is male-centered, particularly around purity of ethics and morals but also in terms of leadership and approaches to problems. *Mea culpa*; the will to power is as strong in me as it is in anyone.

I'm a father of two girls. When our eldest was born she was

colicky and my partner, Sophie, and I rowed a few times over how to help her. I remember holding our new baby and walking away from my wife – I was in tears but no doubt the walking away was intended as a punishment of Sophie. As I stood staring at a waking East London street through those tears, holding my daughter, I felt two almost overwhelming experiences: total conviction – of the ways I'd objectified or mistreated women over the years; and unconditional acceptance – for who I am. Somehow this baby gave me both gifts in one moment. *This*, I thought, *is what is meant by conversion to the grace of God.*

Elsa Tamez, a Latin American activist, published a series of interviews with men about their own machismo. One interviewee, Julio de Santa Ana, brought that conversion event back to me starkly: '… my great teachers in recent years have been my children. They have been unsettling my worldview. The poor [people], my wife, and my children have broken apart the world that I was educated in, a macho world, a world of domination.'[1] Personal vulnerability and a willingness to bear witness to the cost of injustice – one of these does more to transform our world for better than a thousand authoritarian acts for justice.

Introduction

The Call to Peace

It was just a few months after my ordination as a deacon in Gloucester Cathedral. The formality, grandeur and holiness of that event were fresh in my mind. So you probably wouldn't expect me to be lying on the floor in the Cathedral cloisters, surrounded by five angry middle-aged men, and two slightly puzzled police officers who hadn't been expecting to arrest a clerk in holy orders that evening.

I was the least puzzled, I expect, since I knew that disrupting an act of worship at a cathedral was likely to result in some sort of confrontation. I had prepared myself prayerfully for the possibility that I would be bayed at, arrested and potentially assaulted. I didn't expect all three but should never underestimate the violence of a worshipping mob tripped out on an hour of high-octane singing.

Before ordination I had begun to realize that the call on every follower of the way of Jesus is a call to costly prophetic witness. Practicing the compassion of Jesus, a radically inclusive love, was a life of 'experiments in truth', to quote Gandhi. This is no less true when a Zionist preacher tricked his way into a booking in Gloucester Cathedral. He used a local organization as a front in much the same way the British National Party often do because they know most folk would refuse them the booking if they knew who was making it.

This particular preacher of hatred taught that Palestinians' culture didn't exist and that Barack Obama was 'another Hitler'; he encouraged funding for illegal settlements in the Occupied Palestinian Territories and in some web-articles had warned that Jews and Muslims would face a holocaust for not turning to Jesus.

His arrival in our diocese had already brought criticism to the Cathedral leadership who decided to honor the booking. After consulting with the Dean of the Cathedral and with the blessing of the local clergy I went, with another deacon, to interrupt the event with direct but calmly delivered questions and observations. When I did this I was bayed at, heckled, jeered and threatened explicitly with assault. I stood my ground and accused the main speaker of having 'blood on his hands', then pleaded with the congregation not to give him their time and money. For some of the men this was too much for them to hear. They dragged me out; I did not fight but neither did I assist them, trying instead to be a 'dead weight' in their hands. It was only when I got home that I noticed the bruises and realized how fortunate I was not to have been lynched.

Sometimes people think prophetic ministry is glamorous. It isn't. Not only did a member of the congregation threaten me but I was also dragged by five of them out of the nave. I experienced personal threats and libel, on the Internet and in print, and was threatened and assaulted outside my own home.

It was exhausting and isolating and it taught me an important lesson: If you're going to speak out find friends to speak out with you. Some people call this an affinity group: a group of people with more in common than the issue at hand who plan and pray together, agree complementary roles in the struggle for justice, and act with trust and mutual responsibility.

Both before and since the incident in the Cathedral I have been fortunate to be with several affinity groups from whom I've learned a lot. As for the incident itself, aside from the toll it took on my family, it raised an important debate and led to a change of policy in the Cathedral. Extremists would find it much more difficult to exploit the good reputation of the building in the future.

On that occasion I was arrested for a suspected breach of the peace. This got me thinking about what 'peace' might mean to us today. Whose peace did I breach? It wasn't the peace that the Jewish, Christian, and Muslim traditions speak about. This peace, sometimes called *shalom* or *salaam*, was a deep and wide peace that including justice, liberty, healing and wholeness. This peace, the Pax Christi (Peace of Jesus), was a peace I was determined to uphold even if the journey to it included conflict. So I hadn't breached the shalom peace.

The peace that the police were concerned with was the 'Queen's Peace' or Pax Britannica. It was the *pacification* that had been breached. In Jesus' day this was known as the Pax Romana – the Roman Peace. Rome brought about peace with the sword. They forced communities to submit to military domination. Once pacified, a community would give up the best of its resources to the Roman Empire and be kept pacified with a ruthless administration, rewards for puppet-rulers, and military prosecution. It was the Romans that most widely used execution by crucifixion; they would crucify those who breached the Pax Romana in the thousands.

Two things have become clearer to me in the few years that I've been a priest. One is that shalom and pacification are mutually exclusive ways of having peace. The other is that there are many people following Jesus who know that the peace they experience in society isn't the peace that resonates from the biblical witness, the traditions of the Church, or the conviction of the Spirit of God. Yet they don't believe they have the tools to do much about it.

This book looks at why the peace that comes from God is unrecognizable to the peace the systems of the world give, through an analysis of power and engagement with the means to challenge power. It also offers some practical tools, values, and principles that might offer a map – just one of many. We can begin to find the resources, among us, to be the change we want to see in the world. That peace is made possible by the ordinary compassion that we show one another every day. It is a compassion that allows us to be fully human, the more compassionate we are. This is why Jesus was such a threat to the authorities of his day – not because he was 'fully divine', that idea came much later – but because he was so fully and compassionately human.

Chapters one and two take us through some of the spirituality and creativity needed to begin to prophesy both the destruction of the old and the building of the new: the compassion of God. We look at some of the ways philosophers, compassionate activists, and others describe those hard-to-pin-down essences of social organization; what Walter Wink calls 'the Powers'.

Chapter three, 'Sources of Violence', looks at six reasons why we opt for a violent solution to any given crisis, whether personal or national. Chapter four, 'Compassionate Resistance', takes us through compassionate resistance as a biblical and practical option for those with the least power to confront those with the most. We look at the political implications of the love Jesus spoke of and that he and St Paul worked with in their own particular ways.

Chapters five, six, and seven take us to the hard graft of prophetic witness: building a new world in the shell of the old. Jesus spent most of his time mooching around with everyday people, debating with local people of every high and low status, telling stories, offering healing. Without everyday compassion and outpouring of the self, he would have had no authority to speak truth to power, to make any sort of meaningful sacrifice or call others to do the same.

Although the gospels shine most of the limelight on Jesus, he was by no means a lone rebel; his work was invitational and participatory. Jesus was an influential member of a popular movement for revolution and liberation. It was his time among the fishing boats as much as his clashes in Jerusalem that shaped his legacy. We will take a fresh look at some exciting texts to discover an often-overlooked wisdom. We will look at personalism as a radical challenge to individualism. We'll also explore some of the community organizer models that are not directly inspired by the biblical witness but which are transforming our world in ways that those of us in the Church have often forgotten about.

In chapter eight, 'Far from Home', we will use the parable of the lost son to reflect on emotional and political options in relation to our bruised and battered world. We will also look at some practical grassroots movements which are challenging the wisdom of sustainability and progress and may help us make the journey back to a healthy relationship with creation.

In chapter nine, 'The Domination System', we will look at the ways in which the powers distort public opposition. We often receive the impression that we have a healthy democracy that encourages debate. We rarely look at how the parameters of debate are set and who sets them. Chapter nine will be a chance to work through some of those issues.

Chapter ten, 'The Compassion Continuum', gives us the opportunity to look at the way in which Jesus engaged with different people according to where they were in relation to power. This sideways look at Jesus' ability to meet people where they are may offer us some clues for our own communities.

In chapters eleven and twelve we will get to some practical examples, methods, and principles of compassionate resistance. Using the examples of Jesus and Mahatma Gandhi as well as contemporary examples, we will explore how compassionate activism looks in public practice. We will go beyond protest to lamentation and prophecy, and to the propaganda of the Peace of Jesus. For some of us, sometimes this means getting arrested; for others it means a far greater sacrifice. For all of us it promises to be a place of adventure, of self-discovery, of Godly hope.

Time magazine made 'The Protester' their person of the year for 2011. In both wealthy and poorer countries, the 'Occupy!' movement will help define 2011 and shape many ideas and conversations over the coming years. Beginning with the Adbusters collective, and other activist groups inviting US citizens to 'occupy Wall Street', the movement spread all over the world. In the UK there were occupations of public space all over the country but it was the camp at St Paul's Square, near the London Stock Exchange, that grabbed the media attention in Britain. This was partly because of the reaction of the leadership of St Paul's Cathedral. The Cathedral staff took the view that public protest of this kind was inappropriate and unhelpful. They had a long history of debates, articles, and reports on the ethics of the business world at their own St Paul's Institute but no idea has ever emerged from St Paul's Institute that has challenged the systems that create the wealth gaps we see today.

After initial antagonism towards the occupation, St Paul's began to engage with the Occupy movement, especially after the resignation of a senior cleric, Giles Fraser. The desire forcibly to remove the protesters faced public criticism, including from the wider Church. However, St Paul's senior staff further underlined how embedded their culture was with that of the world by appointing Ken Costa, a neo-liberal who uses his vast wealth to push a particular 'brand' of Christianity across the world and had initially called the occupation protesters 'naïve' and their camp 'meaningless'. As one member of another occupation told me, 'People say we don't have any answers, but neither do they; at least we're asking the questions.'

The Occupy movement reminds me of another movement a few decades earlier called Reclaim the Streets which saw groups occupying busy roads and holding parties to highlight the way town planning favors traffic over communities. If we find ways to re-occupy social spaces for new experiments in living abundant lives, we can find new and rediscovered ways of celebrating our humanity and the universe. But by re-occupying and reclaiming, we need to evict those who, as the prophet Isaiah put it, 'join house to house, who add field to field, until there is room for no one but you, and you are left to live alone in the midst of the land!' (Isaiah 5:8). Or as Jesus put it, we need to 'bind up the strongman' before we can occupy the estate (Mark 3:27). This is a spiritual as well as a political re-occupation and eviction process, and this book is an attempt to think through some of the implications of it.

I

Compassionate Imagination

I wish to erase the distinction between a mystical internal and a political external.
Dorothee Soelle

As a teenage Christian I got involved in the more extreme end of the charismatic church: spiritual warfare. I'm not sure if the phrase sounds macho or just weird. We would sing uplifting triumphant songs in chair-less – often windowless – rooms. Cheers, shouts, speaking in the languages of angels, and of course visions of dragons, angels and the occasionally random teacup, would punctuate the agitated air.

Spiritual warfare, as the word 'warfare' suggests, was quite an aggressive affair and rooted in the sort of religious language that rarely makes for justice and peace. Most of us shy away from this kind of spirituality. However, we may be throwing out the baby with the bath water.

For many primitive religions around the world, marginalized by civilized cultures but surviving nonetheless, these shaman-like, charismatic, and ecstatic utterances that I grew up with are common enough. In relation to angels, spirits and demons speaking into the un-named social systems and ethoses, primitive religions speak to the heart and corporate soul of a community.

Jesuit priest Aloysius Pieris tells the story of a Buddhist village in Sri Lanka where he witnessed a possession and exorcism presented as a community event. The aim of the elaborate rite was to expose a deception against the community. In this instance the possessed person reveals that a local grocer has been cheating people by selling them damaged milk cartons at full price – the money-demon is ridiculed and the injustice is exposed, 'calling the devil by its name'. Possession allows the community to name the problem and the community begins the process of becoming free from its power.

These sorts of spiritualities serve a forgotten purpose. They allow oppressed groups to name their oppressor and they help people expose the symptoms of name-able injustices.

Activists are notorious 'doers', as the word suggests, and are often suspicious of too much reflection. I've helped organize five conferences with Christian activists over the past few years and always face the same criticism: 'Why are we talking instead of doing?' It can be a fair criticism. Some of us (okay, me) could happily spend our whole lives theorizing about change while other people are out there experimenting in the reality of it but have set off without a map of the terrain.

A deeply practiced spirituality gives us the strength for those moments of facing down fear and refusing to give violence the last word. Compassionate activism is a recognition that our activism needs to be rooted in our spirituality so that our activity has meaning and can inform future plans. We need, as Gandhi put it, 'experiments in truth'. The purpose of experiments is to test and rework our reality. Spiritual imagination is about what New Testament scholar and activist Walter Wink, following St Paul, calls 'naming the powers'. The word 'powers' is used sometimes in this book in the same way, but more often you will find words like 'systems' and 'structures' to describe the same thing.

Powers of Imagination

So what do we mean by the systems? Have you ever got together with people for something and felt that by acting together you have become something more than a collection of individuals? It is that kind of spiritual reality that we are thinking about here. It is the 'ethos' of the company or the atmosphere you sense at your club; it is your sense of nationhood or what one economist called 'the invisible hand of the marketplace', which more often that not seems to be giving you the finger.

Recently a retired dean of Salisbury Cathedral, Hugh Dickinson, told me how he would get visitors to the building to imagine the angel of the building.

'What would you call the angel of this Cathedral?' he would ask.

'Beauty,' they would almost always reply.

'Yes,' he recounted with a twinkle in his eye, 'it's saying, "Look at me!"'

What Hugh was able to do was show the vanity of the attitudes of those who took pride in the historic building for its own sake and made maintaining it and celebrating it the primary objective of their efforts. Thus they had created a systemic idolatry. The role of the worshipping community was to turn that building back to its primary purpose: the glory of God.

In a letter to the Ephesians, St Paul wrote that our struggle is not against 'flesh and blood' but rather the 'powers and principalities'. Rene Girard takes time to point out how important describing and referencing these powers was to early Church writers.

It is striking how many names the New Testament writers invent to designate these ambiguous entities. They may be called powers 'of this world' then on the other hand 'celestial powers,' as well as 'sovereigns,' 'thrones,' 'dominions,' 'princes of the kingdom of the air,' 'elements of the world,' 'archons,' 'kings,' 'princes of this world,' etc.[2]

For Girard the oscillation between material and spiritual descriptions of reality is deliberate. The two spheres of reality are inseparable. Elsewhere in the Bible these systems are described as angels; we will use an angelic or super-humanized structural image of systems. Angels and demons remain in our culture as embodied descriptions for the systems. They help us to name and challenge them on the level of human interaction. To humanize these entities, to bring them to our level of engagement, is often the first step to wrestling, or binding them up, so that real change can be made in our neighborhoods.

St Paul reminds us that, in a situation of systemic injustice, we cannot just get rid of the person in charge and expect real change. Our response to injustice needs to go deeper and wider than a palace coup. Compassionate activists work together, in solidarity with oppressed people and at times of crisis, seeking God's justice through prayer and action. Compassionate activists nourish discipleship through a growing understanding of how powers should be engaged with.

Compassionate activism is rooted in Paul's radical mysticism. Whatever our style of contemplative study, followers of Jesus develop a compassionate activism that challenges the systemic and institutional injustices. Spirituality can be exciting without being macho and moralizing or fluffy and individualistic. It is a dynamic spirituality that prophetically responds to the brokenness we find, in our world and ourselves.

Compassionate activism involves prayer, imagination, and emotion. It needs a keen and creative analysis of the way social power is structured and broken down. Compassion tends to reveal a political crisis point – a moment of opportunity for 'justice to roll like rivers', as the prophet Amos so dramatically puts it. Authentic compassion also offers the perspective of those at the bottom of the heap while seeing an overarching horizon of systemic reality that needs transforming. So it needs to be rooted in acts of mercy and solidarity with those on the edges of society: they know what it means to live at the sharp end of what the systems are up to.

Biblical Imagination

The Bible often depicts systems as angels. The book of Daniel is a good place to go for an example of the sort of compassionate activism that merges spiritual and political realities. Daniel lived at a time of crisis, a time of exile. He was an administrator at the heart of empire, exiled from his own ransacked city-state to serve imperial masters. To survive he had accommodated to the demands of the powerful while finding ways to subvert or resist the cultural and political hegemony of the Babylonians. When Daniel fasts and prays for his people who are in exile both in Babylon and even in their own city of Jerusalem, the messenger angel describes a contest between the guardian angels of both nations.

The biblical book of Revelation was written in a style not so different from that of Daniel. This too was written in a time of political crisis; when the Jewish and Gentile Christians were displaced and dispersed by an imperial force. The author of Revelation, John of Patmos, was a follower of Jesus at a time when that meant persecution at the hands of a terrible and ambitious Roman Empire. The Roman Empire, like all empires, believed itself to be both benign and God-sent. The Roman Peace, the 'Pax Romana', was its imperial objective. *Pax* is often translated 'peace' but it would be better rendered as 'pacification'.

Empires pacify in order to impose their own orderliness and press home their economic advantages. Angels of empire flatter themselves that they are forces of universal goodness. This self-idealization motivates the expansion and maintenance of its frontiers.

Revelation does not begin with the angels of empire but with the 'angels of the churches'. Putting those systems in order is John's priority. John names and unmasks the angels of the churches and gives a brutal assessment of their virtues and failings.

And to the angel of the church in Laodicea write ... 'I know your works; you are neither cold nor hot. I wish that you were either cold or hot. So, because you are lukewarm, and neither cold nor hot, I am about to spit you out of my mouth. For you say, 'I am rich, I have prospered, and I need nothing.' You do not realize that you are wretched, pitiable, poor, blind, and naked.
(Revelation 3:14–17)

Naming, describing, and redeeming the angels of our churches today is a task essential to the progress of those who want to do their compassionate activism from within them.

Jesus of the gospels (the first four books of the New Testament) follows the same apocalyptic tradition as the authors of Daniel and Revelation. Jesus has a style that is often more subtle and rustic but no less devastating. While he is quoted as referring directly to Satan and to powers, he was just as likely to imagine the systems in ways that aren't so human-like.

Jesus' critique of the systems is illustrated in the cursing of the fig tree. As Jesus and his disciples made their way to the Jerusalem temple they saw a fig tree 'in full leaf'. Jesus went to pick a fig but, finding none, he cursed the tree. What follows is a description of Jesus and the disciples cleansing the temple of moneychangers and traders, and he declares the place a 'den of thieves'. On their journey back the disciples notice that the fig tree has withered. Jesus tells them that, if they trust in God, they can even say to 'this mountain, be thrown into the sea' and it will be.

In Mark's gospel the cursing of the fig tree story acts as a sandwich in which the cleansing of the temple (more of that later) is the filling. This is no coincidence: the cursing of the fig tree was a spiritual insight on the temple action. The withered tree was the aberrant and corrupt cultic practices of the temple elite. To underline his critique Jesus envisions the mountain, an ancient symbol for the security and prosperity of the nation, and claims that, by faith, it can be thrown into the sea (the sea being a symbol of the chaos of pre-creation).

Mark's Jesus wasn't sulking about his disappointment at the lack of a fruity snack for his journey. Jesus was engaged in compassionate activism: a poetic, prophetic insight into the spiritual reality of a system that drove him into action – the cleansing of the temple.

The gospel writers made no distinction between physical and spiritual realities. For them, to tell it how it is means telling it how you understand it to be in the broadest sense. It was only relatively recently that we started separating 'historical' and 'spiritual' as though the latter is fiction and the former is objective fact. In their writing they saw that the angels and demons, principalities and powers, call them what you will, were both structural-institutional realities and things that went beyond physical experience.

It was this understanding that meant Jesus' contemporaries took for granted a correlation between Satan, demons, and political temptations or forces. When Jesus sent the disciples out in twos, healing and proclaiming the compassion of God, he saw 'Satan fall like lightning' (Luke 10:18). When Peter argued with Jesus as to whether his execution was inevitable, he was tempting Jesus to passive or violent intimidation or violent resistance against it. Jesus understood this conversation as a spiritual battle with Satan more than a logistical disagreement between friends (Matthew 16:23). Exploring the biblical imagination like this invites us into the same process, using our own imaginations, inspired by the same spirit of compassion.

Spiritual Imagination

Twenty-first-century followers of Jesus live in times when the systems are more influential than ever but the tools to hand for analyzing and disrupting the work of these spiritual structures are better than ever. Liberal theology, of the twentieth century, grew out of a desire to use historical and literary tools to understand the Bible. Some people have tried, with good intention, to just read the Bible at 'face value'; it sounds like a good idea but the face we value most is usually our own and we read the Bible but we hear our own assumptions reflected back at us. There is no pure reading of any sacred text, only the holy conversation between the readers, the text, and the Spirit. Radical and compassionate spirituality of the twenty-first century is developing out of an ability to use philosophy, psychology, sociology, political studies, and perhaps most importantly the arts to re-invigorate our understanding of our situations.

We can take courage to explore ways in which the arts can help us begin to analyze power and our relationship to it. Compassionate activist Walter Wink sometimes encourages people to draw the angel of their church. Drawing on both their emotional literacy and natural intuition, they step back from and analyze the spiritual health of their spiritual home. I spoke to a couple that found this process provided an important crisis point in their lives. 'My partner and I both drew angels with shrunken bodies and huge swollen heads!' She told me, 'We'd been at that church for decades but when we looked at each other's pictures we knew we had to get out and find a church that was actually doing something instead of just telling us what to think.'

I have encouraged groups to brainstorm metaphors in word or picture form for their parish or district and the results have often surprised them and led them to look differently at how they are. But we need not stop at felt-tip pens: music, dance, sculpture, drama, and many other artistic ways of expressing the inexpressible about a system can lead a group into deeper conversation and more ready ability to critically analyze the institutional structures.

All of this involves a change in worldview from one where the material and spiritual worlds are separate to an understanding of the organic integrity between the spiritual and the physical. In the ancient world there was a complete integrity between the spiritual and material worlds. Greek philosophy separated with more absolute boundaries the pure/theoretical/spiritual and the corrupted/concrete/physical worlds and that fissure stayed with us through to the medieval worldview where heaven was up above and hell down below.

Modern philosophies taught us to compartmentalize or interiorize the spiritual because it had only a limited place in the public realm. Religion became a matter of private conscience, and salvation a matter for the soul. The so-called War of Religions (ca. 1524 to 1648) saw to it that politics motivated by religious convictions was suspect, extremist, and a danger to civil order, and the European enlightenment, which followed quickly after, created the illusions of objectivity and universalized expressions of truth. Any public expression of religion has been made suspect, leaving the ideologies that replaced them: the moral authority of the state as protector, reason as guide, and capitalism as the means of material salvation. Because these ideologies emerged in the western world they have become, for some, the benchmarks of progress and development around the world. In the end what we often think of as a broad spectrum of opinions, or a healthy debate in a democratic system, can keep us safely in quite a narrow arena of ideas.

We need to use the modern tools, the ancient traditions, and our own creative abilities to create a many-faceted link between spiritual and socio-political reality. Knowing what is in the tool kit and when to use which tool for naming and unmasking the powers is the first gift that compassionate activism offers twenty-first-century followers of Jesus.

In this first chapter we have looked at how our imaginations can be made use of to help us better understand one another and the world we live in. In the next chapter we will begin to put that into practice. As we start to imagine the spiritual-social structures in human-like ways, we will see how they have become monsters, false messengers, of our own making. We will be able to see that how we imagine these monsters and messengers shapes how we love our neighbor and how we respond to different uses of power among us.

Building Compassionate Communities

Suggestions for building a compassionate community of resistance where we are:

For Small Groups

Together find metaphors to describe the personality, or psychology, of your group, neighborhood, or organization.

Further Reading

Dorothee Soelle, *The Silent Cry: Mysticism and Resistance*, Augsburg Fortress, 2001.

Walter Wink, *The Powers That Be: Theology for a New Millennium*, Bantam Doubleday Dell, 2000.

Jonathan Ingleby, *Beyond Empire: Postcolonialism and Mission in a Global Context*, AuthorHouse, 2010.

Walter Brueggemann, *Out of Empire*, Abingdon, 2010.

For more information, resources, and a chance to feed back your experiments and ideas, visit: www.compassionistas.net

2

Re-imagining the Systems

When I ask myself seriously what the principalities and powers that rule over me as structural powers claim from me, the answer is that it is my own cowardice that they seek to make use of.
Dorothee Soelle

Our imaginations, and the different techniques of social analysis available to us, are important tools in breaking out of conventional ways of understanding the systems that govern so much of our lives. Our imaginations are powerful; harnessing the power of our imaginations to understand what is happening in the world is rooted in many of the traditions found in religion, not least Judaism and Christianity, where this book has its focus. So, let's see how this re-imagining works out in practice.

We could devote several lifetimes to the academic study of power yet change nothing. However, the careful analysis of institutional structures, through the work of social theorists, can free us up to behave in new ways. Listening to the language of the powerful and how they shape and define meaning on behalf of us all will help us to understand how our own worldviews have been shaped by an exploiting Other. We must understand how the privileged minority keep the working majority in controlled and subdued limits. Our imaginations have become hostage to the imaginings of the powerful.

Below are a few super-humanized imaginings shaped around the three themes of systems as 'monsters', 'messengers', and 'mortals'. We begin to focus on super-humanized imaginings because both social philosophers and scriptural traditions have most often described the social and institutional structures in organic and human-like ways. As monsters they scare, protect and overwhelm us; they even dictate what it means to be us. As messengers they shape the way we send and receive information and invade our spaces, colonizing the gaps in between the person and their experiences. As mortals they are revealed as temporary, flawed; they have their final destruction built into their DNA.

Systems as Monsters

Super-humanizations of society are often gigantic or exaggerated, but deeply flawed, human forms. A useful way to describe the systems is as monsters, even if those who first imagined and proposed them did not see them as monstrous.

Colonial and postcolonial Indian society humanize social reality through the ancient-but-evolving caste system. The Hindu myth, found in the Rig Veda, and exploited by colonialists and Indian nationalists, tells the story of how humans were created from the head, arms, stomach, and feet of the giant, Purusha. Those created from the head were the priestly families, then those from the shoulders and arms were the warriors; those made from the stomach were the merchants; those made from the feet were the servants. This was considered a natural and organic order that should not be resisted. Those who transgress these boundaries, through racial descent or breaking marriage taboos, are called outcastes and untouchables. To many people, this mythology serves as a map for how they understand the world even today when legislation claims to have abolished the caste system over sixty years ago.

Medieval European imaginations regarded society in much the same way. For a medieval peasant it would have been an accepted part of the universe that the lord – who is the stomach in the analogy of the body – does not labor since hands and feet do the grafting to satisfy the body. To cut out the stomach would be a gruesome and crazy act of suicide; likewise the head. So the role of the elite was sanctioned and naturalized by the analogy. Removing privilege was a perversion: dangerously unnatural.

In the modern, capitalist era, as the state got bigger, society was shrunk to a unit of one. Through centuries of Christian apologetics that 'one' was seen as 'fallen': naturally evil and needing to be restrained and redeemed. This assumption about human identity was vital to the shaping of the monster of modern capitalist states.

Because individualism replaced the idea of society as a body of people, the monster had to be projected onto some external idea in order to survive into the consciousness of this era. It did so with the help of people like the philosopher Thomas Hobbes.

Hobbes wrote, with all the untested certainty that only a life of privilege can bring, that primitive people lived 'short, nasty, and brutish' lives. Hobbes had an unquestioned assumption, still rarely put under the spotlight. Hobbes was a deeply thinking reformer of religion who tried to sort out, in a world where much of the old assumptions were being questioned, how religion could survive in a world where reason was so highly valued.

Hobbes sought to protect religion by confirming its role in private belief that must be kept in check by the divinely appointed authority of the state. Thus the state could retain its privileged place, God could remain the ultimate authority, and religion could be prevalent but kept under control. Hobbes also believed that humans are inherently selfish and violent. The idea of a human society unchecked by fear of punishment from some more powerful authority must have been a terrible threat. Hobbes had no proof of this theory but it remains implicit in western societies and the places that Europeans colonized around the world.

Hobbes didn't invent the idea of humans being born evil; early Christian thinkers had seen to that. But he wrote a book called *Leviathan* in which he describes fallen human nature and the need to protect these mean creatures from destroying one another. What Hobbes had in mind was a theoretically benign and fair power capable of greater violence than any person, maintaining peace through threat of force. This was a justification for governments run as sophisticated protection rackets; offering security, threats, and extortion. It was the Pax Romana all over again.

Broadly speaking, it is this view of humanity as being predisposed to violence and of the role of states as protecting us from ourselves and from others like us 'abroad' that western societies have inherited. Because we cannot be trusted to govern ourselves, justice and rule-making have been contracted from personal relationship to an impersonal political elite. Different states have their own ways of making individuals feel that they have a small but important part to play in the way states govern. In Britain we have a first-past-the-post system which validates the votes of the majority, usually for someone representing third-party interests – the lobbies that fund the political parties – and does not recognize in any way the views of those who either don't vote or don't vote for the winner. The MPs and those in the systems they work from, in turn, answer, not to the electorate, whose involvement is infrequent and unorganized, but to those with the money and influence that allows them to shape public opinions and individual decision-makers. The state's fundamental mission statement is to prevent humans from destroying one another. But why do we want to destroy one another? Capitalism relies on us thinking of ourselves as individuals, rather than communities, and reliant on power and property, rather than the love of our neighbor. Capitalism makes us brutish and the state is the brute that keeps our brutishness in check while propping up capitalist systems and ideas.

Since the late 1940s we could add to Leviathan the role of carer. The term 'nanny state' has become a useful pejorative term for those wanting to criticize the way the national structures are said to create dependency among individuals in society by offering them anonymous professional care rather than care that comes through their own community. Capitalism requires a flexible workforce with people in many professions who must be ready to change where they live: to leave their community. Sociologists often call this 'social mobility' because the wealthier a person is, the more likely they are to be able to move house. But the arrangement is primarily to the benefit of the employer who requires the move, not vice versa. So a national welfare system has been vital in a world where capitalism has eroded community through so-called 'social mobility'. The 'nanny state' is both a fix and a symptom of a capitalist economy.

But now we have at least two images working in our collective psyche as though they are natural: the violent protector and the dispassionate carer. If you can imagine Godzilla in an A-line dress and wimple we have a pretty good imagining of the Power that watches over the British nation.

The nanny-monster image is only part of the picture but, as we begin to visualize the system, we begin to understand our relationship to it and how we might respond. To go deeper and perhaps closer to our current understanding of institutional structures, we have to think beyond national and geographical government toward what political philosopher Raj Patel calls 'The Corporation'. The word 'corporation' literally means 'the body' and the term suits both the spiritual reality and legal status of national and international companies but particularly those owned by shareholders; these companies are legally obliged to put profit ahead of ethics.

Corporations, according to Patel, can be accurately diagnosed as psychopaths. They are antisocial, deceitful, short-term-minded, aggressive, reckless in regard to the safety of others, irresponsible and lacking in remorse. Patel gives the example of the agricultural monster that is Monsanto.

For decades, Monsanto employees suppressed knowledge about what happened when they dumped toxic waste from their Anniston, Alabama, plant into local streams – the fish died within ten seconds, spurting blood and shedding skin. A representative from Monsanto's spin-off, Solutia, said ... 'If you put it all in context, I think we've got nothing to be ashamed of.'[3]

It is apparent that those who head up corporations don't always take personal responsibility for what the corporations are up to. Patel goes on to point out that such corporations often have legal standing and rights as persons. These monsters have greater protection in law than persons could ever hope to have with few sanctions.[4] Regional laws are recognizing monsters as persons. Compassionate activists need to name and expose these idols and begin to challenge the arrogance and self-will of these transnational monsters.

The few examples above show us that imagining the systems can tell us more than material descriptions can. Finding imaginative ways to name these monsters helps us discover how we intuit and emotionally respond to them. It also shows us how our own behaviors are linked to theirs. Imagination is a tool of the person and community refusing to follow a pre-determined outcome. Our own imagination can be the source of truths we didn't know we were capable of articulating about our selves and our world.

The self-justifying monsters offer security but at the price of perpetual anxiety. A monster can be an amoral, but legally protected, bully whose greedy arms reach beyond national borders and even into people's homes. The monsters we feed, worship, defend, and even honor in our secular and religious liturgies are often the kind of beings we would not want to meet in a dark alley; most of us would probably want them locked up with the key thrown away. Yet because of our refusal to see them as idols we allow them to thrive and bask in our adoration.

So we reward genetically modifying, patent-hungry monsters like Monsanto, even though they create starvation, slavery, and environmental disaster, because they dazzle us with the promise of technological and economic salvation. We shop till we drop because Marks and Spencer tell us that there is a lifestyle attached to the sweater we buy. We sacrifice the lives of our military because the oil and gas-guzzling monsters – which isn't only the oil industry but all systems dependent on fossil fuels – demand that we feed them ever more of the earth's natural resources. We are told they live to serve us but deep down we all know that we live to serve them. The monsters are our masters and naming them is the first step to defeating them. The monsters are false gods and describing them is the first step to blaspheming against them.

Systems as Messengers

We turn our attention now to the systems as messengers, which is what the word 'angel' literally means. We will consider how and why these messengers shape our imaginations and behaviors with or without our permission.

The ways in which messages are transmitted are increasingly complex and it is the method as much as the message that matters. Jacques Ellul, a political philosopher known for his analysis of the technological society, describes brilliantly the way technology dominates and how we receive information.

Walking or driving in an SUV, even if to the same place, sends a different message. Listening to a story told around a fire or watching an on-screen adaptation alters both the content and the experience of it. Technology is the medium by which we interact with many of our experiences of the world around us. It is a mediator of information but as such it cannot be value-neutral. The way we choose to receive a message is in itself a message. In Britain we once had thriving local economies. But some important technological advancement has changed all that. Stores can be bigger and built more cheaply in a separate place from neighborhoods. Some of the savings are passed on but the cost of this change is mostly borne by the person buying stuff who often needs to buy a car, pay for the petrol, and drive to the place where stuff is bought. This could be framed as increased consumer choice and a boom to the economy. In reality it decreases choice because a few large multinational businesses replace lots of small ones. But we give in to this change as though it is both wanted and life enhancing, perhaps because it is made possible by technological progress. And progress sounds like a good thing. Technology self-justifies when we organize our lives around technological advancements rather than allowing our real needs to shape which techniques or technologies are useful. The way I choose to experience the natural world, or indeed put distance between creation and me, reinforces a message about who I am in relation to everything else. So we must begin by looking at the essence of communication.

Let's start with the early human attempts to put technological distance between humanity and the earth: the shift from the human who dug, plucked and gripped the earth with bare hands to the plough-bearing human. Immediately there is a techno-logical distance between us and all else that God calls 'good'. We forget what soil smells like and feels like; we forget how fully alive a clod of earth is. From now on, the earth is communicated to us through plough and sickle and the increasingly distancing technologies that we experience today. For many urban centers, creation is now mediated through supermarkets; we have little recourse to experience the earth any more closely than that.

Our experience of the ground is mediated by technology, and the means of knowing the earth – the tools – is the message itself: a message of domination and control. From that moment the gap has widened exponentially as we denude the ground and replenish it with fossil-fuel-based fertilizers and pesticides. We destroy increasing amounts of beautiful healthy wilderness in order to subdue, simplify and profit from the soil.

On Easter eve, at Saint Katharine's Church, a small group

gathers after nightfall. We sit in the still darkness of our church: not new enough to be functional, not old enough to be listed. We can barely see one another's face but our voices carry well in the night air. 'So how does our story begin?' says Jeni, the rector. 'It begins in a garden,' comes the first offer. 'No, with chaos then a garden,' interjects another. We don't build up the story from the book; many of us rarely read books. But we build the story, as it matters to us in that moment in that community. Before we had books and telly we would tell one another our stories. Storytelling is a community affair; even if there is a storyteller the intimacy invites participation. Story, song, drama were predominantly participative; news was told and recast outside of events it referred to, changing the value of the original event to reflect the over-arching stories that the community held dear.

We can hear echoes of this world in some of the older texts in the Bible. The story of resistance to empire in Daniel chapter 3, for example, lends itself to oral telling with the humorous repetition of the list of instruments, mocking the grandeur of the king: 'Therefore, as soon as all the peoples heard the sound of the horn, pipe, lyre, trigon, harp, drum, and entire musical ensemble, all the peoples, nations, and languages fell down and worshipped the golden statue that King Nebuchadnezzar had set up.' Whenever I read it I can imagine it told in an open courtyard with the listeners waiting eagerly to help the storyteller remember the list each time it weaves into the tale.

Amongst the Dalit and Tribal communities of India, oral storytelling remains a popular rural event nudged aside only for the epic Indian movie culture. Once, when staying in the tribal belt jungles of Gujarat, I was walking to a friend's home when we came across a common scene in Indian villages. An outdoor cinema with the screen projected onto the largest whitewashed wall available. The film would last around four hours but the end of it brought about not a shuffling off to bed but the corporate retelling and reshaping of the film in excited and imaginative co-opting. The technology served one purpose but it could not replace the attraction of friends participating in their own storytelling. In this process, new messages get scrutinized by the old and may work their way into folklore, or not, depending on the response of the community.

Although storytelling is not a formal part of the lives of many western communities, even in a British city flat someone will be telling a story and others will be joining, or listening, in. These retellings, wherever and whenever they occur, are textured and colored-in by the voices, perspectives, and interjections. They are neither neat nor can they be authentically lifted out of the telling and onto the page of a book without first tidying away the bit of the telling that brings them to life.

The immediacy and purity of mass media, on the other hand, sterilizes the story process, producing realities that claim objectivity but are still framed. The carefully scripted news and views of the mass media is colored-in by those who dominate those industries.

When two planes hit tower blocks in New York killing around 3,000 people, half a dozen images were sterilized of first-hand experience and political complexity and repeated on TV screens and computers around the world, until the single event felt like *War of the Worlds*. It became a thing of propaganda fiction. We watched the same images over and over as though we were being given raw facts rather than a cynically framed reality. The framing was in the repetition of the images, the cues given by reporters, and the bringing of the terror into the otherwise safe-space of the living room. The same 'objective' technology chooses not to show us endless images of children dying of preventable diseases; militarized bulldozers destroying civilian homes day after day; the effects of Morgan Stanley investments on Chinese rural life because these events offer the sort of critique of technology that the technological systems cannot bear.

Technology elbows its way into the space between humans

and one another but also the space between humanity and the rest of nature. We appear strange to one another and strangers to the natural world. Everyone and everything becomes 'other': suspect and dangerous, needing to be trapped, tamed or destroyed. There is sacredness about the space between one spark of divinity and another as they meet in recognition; any technical mediation between the two can only offer a counterfeit approximation to personal communication.

Perhaps this is why an exhausted office worker might summon up the energy to dig the garden, tend the allotment, or walk the dog. The industrial process of partitioning working people away from the meaning of their work accelerated with industrial techniques; we no longer understand much of the work that we do. We are given responsibility without power and labor without a day of rest. Before we lie down at night we may feel that longing to get a little of the humus (soil) back in our humanity (soul). We all want a little returning to the garden of our autonomy. We want to do something with as few go-betweens of technology as possible.

In 2001, journalist, author, and political activist Naomi Klein captured the imagination of a generation with her book *No Logo*. In it she describes the origins and development of corporate branding. She relates some of the impact of branding, and ways in which people around the world have resisted the messages of the corporations eager to keep their brand at the forefront of our minds.

Every year companies spend billions investing their logos, jingles, and catchphrases with subconscious meaning. Anyone who was taken for a 'Happy Meal' as a special treat when they were young and remembers walking out blissed-out with a cheap toy and a limp warm burger knows the power of branding. The feelings they experience when they see a big yellow 'M' will probably stay with them for their whole lives, nudging their behavior when they are tired of driving on the motorway or their own children are acting up. Corporations don't spend billions of dollars on advertising to inform, but rather to direct choice.

Always behind the brands lies another story and an entirely different set of values and aspirations. The purpose of the message is not to convey truth but to encourage an emotional, political, and economic attachment to what lies behind the brand. Brands want loyalty and obedience. Breaking this illusion is the beginning of spiritual unrest and social change.

The Inevitable Collapse of Unjust Structures

However overwhelming they seem, all unjust structures collapse eventually. Understanding how structures are propped up is only useful if it helps us challenge and overthrow them, or negate them out of existence.

Gene Sharp uses a fourteenth-century Chinese parable he calls 'The Monkey Master' to describe the real relationship between people and the ultimate illusion: that of 'power over'.

> In the feudal state of Chu an old man survived by keeping monkeys in his service. The people of Chu called him 'ju gong' (monkey master). Each morning, the old man would assemble the monkeys in his courtyard, and order the eldest one to lead the others to the mountains to gather fruits from bushes and trees. It was the rule that each monkey had to give one-tenth of his collection to the old man. Those who failed to do so would be ruthlessly flogged. All the monkeys suffered bitterly, but dared not complain.[5]

Creating a sense of duty and dependency keeps us in thrall to the institutional structures that dictate so much of the quality of our being alive and experience of life. But the good news is that these systems thrive on a paper-thin premise of authority.

One day, a small monkey asked the other monkeys: 'Did the

old man plant all the fruit trees and bushes?' The others said: 'No, they grew naturally.' The small monkey further asked: 'Can't we take the fruits without the old man's permission?' The others replied: 'Yes, we all can.' The small monkey continued: 'Then, why should we depend on the old man; why must we all serve him?' Before the small monkey was able to finish his statement, all the monkeys suddenly became enlightened and awakened. On the same night, watching that the old man had fallen asleep, the monkeys tore down all the barricades of the stockade in which they were confined, and destroyed the stockade entirely. They also took the fruits the old man had in storage, brought all with them to the woods, and never returned. The old man finally died of starvation. Yu-li-zi says, 'Some men in the world rule their people by tricks and not by righteous principles. Aren't they just like the monkey master? They are not aware of their muddlehead-edness. As soon as their people become enlightened, their tricks no longer work.'[6]

Sharp's word 'muddleheadedness' describes so simply the goal of the systems: in order for systems to fool us into worshipping them, they must colonize the means of communication and take authority over what we do and how we feel.

Sharp is globally acknowledged as a leader in the study of nonviolent removal of authoritarian systems. He lists seventeen weaknesses of a dictatorship that can be instructive in any analysis of authoritarian power. Below are just a few, adapted for clarity:

- They require the co-operation of many groups and institutions.
- Routine systems become slow to adapt to popular reactions.
- The desire of elites to please rulers leads to self-censoring

of bad news.

- Brands, heavily invested, can be suddenly corrupted.
- Ideological narrowness can lead to big mistakes.
- People get fed up with the increasingly negative effects of the system.
- The more centralized the decision-making, the harder it is for the system to act efficiently.

These select observations remind us that maintaining power does not come naturally. Each system relies on a huge and complicated amount of force to retain its status quo, let alone consolidate and expand. Totalitarianism doesn't come easy, and it is vulnerable at every side to compromise and corruption.

Let's unpack the last of these bullet points: 'The more centralized the decision-making, the harder it is for the system to act efficiently.' To help us we can turn to a fascinating and practical analogy from Julian Assange, the founder of the news agency Wikileaks. For this analogy we'll need to rummage around in the shed for a large sheet of wood, some nails and a hammer, and a long ball of string. Have you got all that? Good. If not, feel free to borrow them from a neighbor.

Now hammer the nails into the wood; it doesn't matter where, just have fun hitting them in but leave enough space to wind the string around the top of each nail. Imagine that one of the nails is the center of power and all the nails connect back to this one nail through connections made by the bits of string. Some of the connections are strong so you will need to pass the string back and forth a few times; these are lines of communication that are regularly used. Other connections are rarely used.

Oppressive regimes maintain their authority by restricting the amount of information sent and received. They cannot allow the whole truth to be known, even within their own system of networks. If we wanted to close down such a system we would need to cut all those bits of string. This is a practical impossibility.

Assange argues that it is far better to encourage the system to shut down its own lines of communication by generating so many information leaks into the public domain that those at the center cannot trust the channels of communication and voluntarily close them down. Jesus puts it like this: 'A house divided against itself cannot stand' (Matthew 12:25).

Compassionate activism is the ability to discover the shadowy souls of the systems, by will of the collective imagination, in order to better understand the characters, mechanisms, and flaws that they possess. Systems are both social institutions and spiritual bodies that can be named and blasphemed against or carelessly worshipped. They are both the message and the means of communication that keeps us ready and willing to work to their ends rather than the common good. Finally they are mortal in that they can be transformed, or destroyed while we set about imagining and building the grassroots alternatives.

Unjust systems are like huge machines putting natural materials under immense pressure. The voluntary sector, including churches, often takes the role of the steam valve – giving vent to frustration, offering pastoral care to those who get crushed or squeezed out – an important role, no doubt. However, we also need to be spanners in the works, grinding the cogs to a halt and calling a walk-out on the mass production of social and spiritual inequality: proclaiming release to the captives and the compassion of God among us.

We have begun to sketch out an imaginative and spiritual response to the unjust structures that order so much of our lives. Just by doing this, and especially as we do it together, we become more awake to the oppression and violence that we either are responsible for or experience. It is understandable that we might respond with either a fatalistic helplessness or the sort of panicked and moral anger that demands justice. So before we go much further down this road, we need to explore the sources of violence and the impact they have on struggles for justice. It is not enough to either embrace or dismiss the violence within and around us. We must find out where it is coming from and where it leads. In the next chapter we will explore six sources of violence; as you read on you may be able to recognize them as part of your story or find other sources of violence not mentioned in this book. But you are invited to use the opportunity to explore your relationship with that common experience of violence.

The sources we will look at are deference to authority, fear, principally of death, helplessness in the face of overwhelming situations that we have not got the skills to respond to, a worldview that reinforces the idea that the good always win, the scapegoating mechanism that allows us to choose and abuse victims for the sake of social pacification, and an inhumanity that comes from being strangers to the universe we used to call home.

Building Compassionate Communities

Suggestions for building a compassionate community of resistance where we are:

For Small Groups

Imagine an unjust structure as an inverted triangle balanced on a single point but propped up by many columns. Label the triangle and begin to identify and label the individual columns that hold that structure up.

Further Reading

Naomi Klein, *No Logo*, Fourth Estate, 2000.

Simon Barrow and Jonathan Bartley (eds), *Consuming Passion: Why the Killing of Jesus Really Matters*, DLT, 2005.

Raj Patel, *The Value of Nothing: How to Reshape Market Society and Redefine Democracy*, Portobello, 2009.

Karl Marx, *Capital*, Create Space, 2010.

William T. Cavanaugh, *The Myth of Religious Violence: Secular*

Ideology and the Roots of Modern Conflict, OUP, 2009.

For more information, resources, and a chance to feed back your experiments and ideas, visit: www.compassionistas.net

3

Sources of Violence

More than anything else, violence must hide itself in the form of imperatives, such as security, protection, technological necessity, public order, or defensive measures.
Dorothee Soelle

We have re-imagined social systems as both monsters and messengers. The monsters reinforce the idea that violence is inevitable, natural, and neutral. It is only immoral to be violent if your violence is out of the context of the systems that maintain order. The systems act as messengers that put a gap between you and me taking over many of the ways we communicate and shaping our opinions. One of the ways we have been shaped by unjust systems is in relation to violence. It is to the place of violence in creation that we turn now.

Violence is that which works to reduce our humanity. This may be physical force, but not all force is violent. It may be any form of coercion that forces one to adopt a position of power over another.

Violence is a dominant theme through both the Old Testament and the New Testament. But violence is not the last word even if much of Christian witness might lead us to believe that God's violence is a moral and practical option.

In the Old Testament we often read of a wrathful even genocidal God: one minute sending in agents to destroy everything in a given area (Isaiah 13:15–18) and the next moment espousing love and showering the object of affection with gifts and blessings (Isaiah 14:1–2). In this concept of God, love and violence go hand in glove without a trace of irony (Psalm 136:10).

The prophets, to whom we turn for visions of justice, and

mercy, are rarely any gentler than the Judges, Kings, and Psalmists. We have already heard from Isaiah's God but Elisha's temper and cruelty is hideous yet sanctioned by the divine. The comical brutality is narrated when Elisha was confronted by children calling him 'Baldy' and responded by getting God to set bears on them, murdering forty-two of them (2 Kings 2:23–24).

Equally, the New Testament has some difficult passages: St Paul is happy to hand believers to Satan for the destruction of their bodies (1 Corinthians 5:5); Jesus promises worse than fire and brimstone from above (Matthew 10:15). Meanwhile, in the Acts of the Apostles a financial vanity on the part of some new believers leads to their immediate execution directly by God (Acts 5:1–11). This is not the stuff of 'gentle Jesus meek and mild'.

We need to understand what the motivators of violence are. Individually and collectively people act with great compassion and sacrifice but also with terrible inhumanity. It's right that we ask 'Why?' Here are six potential sources of violence; perhaps you can think of others?

1 Deference
2 Fear
3 Helplessness
4 Worldview
5 Scapegoating
6 Inhumanity

Deference

First let's look at deference: our attitude to authority figures and our keenness to defer to them in all matters including those that guide our moral compass. Stanley Milgram, an American psychologist, wanted to know how far ordinary people would be willing to go beyond their usual moral limits, when deferring to an authority figure.

Milgram set up a simple yet profoundly significant experiment. Two people would face one another either side of a glass screen. One had tasks to teach the other and a panel of buttons. The second was attached to electrodes and had a few buttons to register the degree of pain felt. The second was, in fact, an actor and would pretend to be painfully shocked as the 'teacher' – the real subject of the experiment – pressed the buttons the teacher believed she or he increased the intensity of the shock each time the other person failed a test.

As the screams of anguish became more distressing, many people who took part would hesitate and yet they would press on past what they thought were dangerous levels of electric treatment because they were assured by an authority figure in a lab coat that they would not be held responsible.

Many of us have been taught from early years to discern right from wrong based on rewards and punishments. We become good people but our moral compass is external to us. We know when we are being good because we are being rewarded by an authority figure and we know when we are being bad because we feel like we have let down the person in charge and ultimately those who brought us up. I am not just talking about parents who smack here but rather all attempts to coerce people into being good instead of helping one another to connect with our own real needs and those of others.

Spirituality anchors the activist in recognition that the divine spark animates all creation, making responsibility personal and wellbeing corporate. A compassionate activist's only authority is the One, referred to by St John as 'Love', who is discerned with humility and mutual aid. Any other authority needs to be held in permanent suspicion relative to this Love.

Fear

Our second source of violence is fear. Adrenalin and fear are important factors that can lead us to violence. Fear is rooted in anxiety about not having our basic needs met. This is ultimately a fear of dehumanization and death. Most of the time, preserving my own life is a useful instinct. But the ability to override that instinct with a trust that all life is held in God alters the control we have over our responses to danger radically. Those who lose their life will save it while those who save their own lives may lose their humanity.

The possibility of seeing beyond fight or flight into a third option of nonviolent resistance can be opened up with a disciplined rhythm of prayer in community. This is because doing the work of spiritual contemplation together changes us.

Bringing our liturgical life into the public square – as we shall see in later chapters – turns our corporate contemplation into something new. Nothing changed my relationship to my community's prayer book more than praying it in a police cell. Nothing changed my experience of the Psalms more than saying them in the shadow of a nuclear weapons factory. Nothing changed my experience of the book of Lamentations more than saying them in the city center interspersed with the names of the casualties of war.

By understanding and speaking out our needs and by hearing with compassion the needs of others, we learn the source of both our fear and our love for others. The Bible allows the whole cacophony of voices room to speak: from the most powerful to the least. In hearing this rich heritage and all the voices of those whose needs remain unmet in our own time, we face up to fear in ourselves and in others. Perfect understanding leads us to perfect love and perfect love casts out all fear.

Silliness plays a part as well. As a ten-year-old I used to love fighting and would sometimes have to sneak into the house to wash off the blood. But as I got older so my fear grew. I will always remember the day I avoided a bloody exchange outside a pub when I was sixteen. A good friend and I had a disagreement over a girl we both liked. We were in a pub and worse for wear.

What started out as a quiet argument was managed by the baying crowd into a stand-off on the pavement outside.

We stood opposite each other glaring; each daring the other to move forward and attack. We goaded each other as the crowd of our peers stood around shouting 'Fight! Fight! Fight!...' In a moment of sobriety I became more aware of the crowd than of my opponent. I realized I didn't really want to fight but was now too afraid to back down. I knew the argument was unhelpful but the time for words seemed to have vanished. I needed somehow to diffuse the situation.

I still don't quite know how it came to me: I unclenched my little fists and grabbed my own ears, making them stick out, while puffing up my cheeks and sticking out my tongue. It was my 'Pob' impression; I've since seen it in photos taken around the same time. My opposite number couldn't help laughing, at which point we shook hands and he bought me a pint – much to the disappointment of the crowd who weren't quite sure what had happened. Finding a way over the other side of fear often involves being creative and daring in ways that, aside from the moment of inspiration, is often hard to plan.

Worldview

What Walter Wink calls 'the myth of redemptive violence' is the commonly held belief, hugely invested in, that violence not only saves us but that it is an important measure of moral rightness. Our whole worldview is shaped by a belief in the myth of redemptive violence, which we often give in to, either in our thinking or on an emotional level. We act out of this belief when we act without stopping to ask ourselves which over-arching story of how the world works is guiding us.

From children's cartoon characters (Popeye, The Incredibles, Superman), to blockbusting films (*Kung Fu Panda*, *X-Men*), western culture has been saturated with the idea that those who win in battle are thus proven to be morally superior. The underlying belief is that the universe, or the divine, is inclined to favor the righteous in battle so you know whose side good/God is on by seeing who claims victory.

This belief has a number of antisocial effects. It inclines us only to listen to the victor's version of history. There is an ancient African proverb: 'Until the lions have their historians, tales of the hunt shall always glorify the hunter.' This refusal to hear critical voices in relation to a conflict opens us up to the idea of conflict in the future.

Those who are victorious make a moral claim on those who believe in the myth of redemptive violence: the world would be a worse place had they lost, according to their telling of the tale, and allegiance to them in the future is vital for keeping further evils at bay.

The worldview that violence saves us determines more of our actions than we might realize. From styles of parenting and leadership, through reward and punishment, to our seemingly instinctive desire to call the police who carry with them the constant threat of violence in order to protect our property and person, we rely daily on the availability of saving violence. Our taxes pay for the military; our parades and religions celebrate the honorable dead. We have a cult of the myth of redemptive violence that's so all pervasive that, like most all-pervasive myths, we rarely notice its influence.

Helplessness

For a couple of years I lived in East London. I loved the small community of social housing tower blocks we lived in. It had its challenges as most communities do. Communal bins were regularly set alight for a while and we would wake up in the night with our bedroom full of smoke, for example, or our neighbors would threaten one another with knives. But we got involved in the residential committee and the local church and got to know everyone on the ground floor fairly quickly.

But the area had a reputation for trouble and the police were keen to show that they were doing their bit. Just before we arrived a sign was put up facing our bedroom window that said, 'Warning: Anti-Social Behaviour is an Offence'. We didn't like opening our curtains to that each morning so we changed it: 'Warning: Love one another'. Much better!

But one day it all went wrong. A neighbor decided to antagonize a guest at our house and stole his camera. The next day we went over to try and settle things. We were confronted by bizarre claims being made against us as well as threats of blackmail. My wife and I were threatened and sworn at as we left the house over the coming days and weeks, and going home was difficult.

I resisted calling the police at first but, under pressure from others, finally did so. They came over, listened, had a chuckle, and were generally useless. We asked for mediation but they said we could press charges or not. We chose instead to find every opportunity to show compassion. Eventually they started acting like nothing had happened. Then one evening, when both the adults had either drunk heavily, taken a lot of coke, or both, one, standing outside her home, frightened to go back in, broke down and confessed everything. In the weeks and months around this event we relied on the love and support of neighbors and our residents' group who helped us through with good humor and advice.

Reflecting back on this incident, I wondered what had caused me to phone the police. I knew they had nothing to offer the situation. I wondered if there was a deeply held conviction, going back to my childhood, that the police are there to protect me from baddies. But primarily there was an acute feeling of helplessness. The community I lived in had no means of dealing with tensions between neighbors without reference to state authorities. We had forgotten how to constructively hold one another to account and so, childlike, we ran to an external enforceable authority in times of internal conflict.

It takes a number of incidents of police intervention, whether as victim or offender, for us to lose our childlike trust in state-sponsored penalties and to begin to wonder if there might be better ways of feeling secure. But meanwhile we feel helpless.

Most of all, whether we choose to make use of protective, or saving, violence for ourselves, we are constantly confronted by the shadow of violence. A source of violence is our inability to see nonviolent options that work for us. In a sense this is what this whole book is about: moving out of helplessness to a compassionate confidence in God's wonderful gift of human community.

We have a whole host of legal violent options at our disposal; police, courts, parents and carers, and prisons being the most obvious. Governments throw huge amounts of money at a penal system of social ordering and at the study of war for the safeguarding of the state. Nation states, who rely on our belief that violence is our savior, keep us dependent on their protection from external threat. Because of this we are de-skilled in nonviolent options, and even the way we talk to one another becomes about reward and punishment or the threat of violence.

We have been schooled to think that the only choice in most situations of conflict is fight or flight, so rather than assess the moral implications we simply work out the likely outcome and duck and dive accordingly.

Of course this isn't the whole story; our true human nature pokes through sometimes with creative solutions and win-win opportunities but these are the exception to the norm.

Scapegoating

Another source of violence is scapegoating. Social philosopher Rene Girard describes this as rooted in conflicts that naturally arise when we compete with those we admire. Imagine two lads who play constantly together and share all interests bar none. They, fish, climb, play, and fight together and of course support the same football team. One day one of them meets a girl; she is adorable and he adores her. He tells his best friend how beautiful, intelligent and funny she is and the friend is keen to share in his pal's enthusiasm.

The friend is so keen to be like his best friend in all things that pretty soon he too is in love with the girl. It is at this point that all hell breaks loose and for the first time these firm friends fall out with each other. It scares them and both hope to resolve their dispute, but they are unwilling or unable to find the source of it. Instead, they seek an outsider to be the target of their anger. The girl, whose arrival on the scene coincided with the conflict, is the obvious choice. She must be blamed in order to preserve the 'peace' between the friends.

Scaled up, the same can be true of any community where identification with one another's desires leads to an inter-communal conflict, which is resolved either by the group destroying itself in revenge or destroying a symbolic outsider. The group usually chooses the outsider rather than face deeper internal issues.

There is an ancient tradition both within and beyond the biblical text of this process. In the Hebrew Scriptures there is a description of a goat being chosen each year to bear the sins of the whole community and be exiled: sent into the wilderness. All this makes for peace but it is a false peace because it is temporary and because it does not deal with the cause of conflict and in the process creates innocent victims.

Identifying the likely scapegoats in our societies and standing alongside them, equipping our communities with means of identifying and working through the causes of conflict, is the stuff of the good news of Jesus. Jesus after all was an innocent victim made to pay for the sins of the system but vindicated by a resurrecting God who refused the sacrificial offering of the 'Human One' as Jesus called himself (Matthew 26:63–64) and turned the scapegoating world upside down. In telling the story of a resurrected innocent victim, the gospel writers bring to the forefront a story that has long been part of the Jewish tradition: that it is the outsider, the scapegoat, the one who is beyond care that directs us to the true compassionate justice of God.

Inhumanity

Our final source of violence is the inhumanity that results from our disconnection with the world outside ourselves. The more distant we are from a meaningful relationship with creation, the more likely we are to act impersonally and oppressively toward it. The more impersonally and oppressively we act, the more numb becomes our connection to the universe, robbing us of our humanity and of a meaningful relationship. This truth is an important corollary to any belief that there are two groups: victims of oppression and those who benefit from it. In the deepest sense of 'human being' all of us are victims of oppression, whether we are the initiators or the receivers of violence. No wonder Jesus told us to love our enemy; any other advice would play into our sense of inhumanity and lead only to more violence and greater estrangement.

My grandmother on my mother's side was 'a Theobald' and the Theobalds were said to be so closely identified with one another that 'if you kicked one, they all limped'. Whether this was true or not (I never tested the theory) it shows an ability to identify the others with the one person. It showed connectedness on a manageable scale. It also created mutual aid and discouraged internal conflict because what was good for one was seen as good for all. Such a narrow definition of our unity is problematic in many ways but, scaled up to the whole universe, it lets us in on a wholly different spiritual perspective.

A lack of personalization makes violence or oppression more likely because we cannot see the connection between our violence and the harm we do ourselves. We do not automatically notice our humanity being diminished every time we diminish the other person. This is why, below, a whole chapter is committed to explore the meaning of personalism. Being a person and being compassionate are indivisible as much as being dehumanized and lacking compassion go together too.

The same is true in our lack of connection with creation. If we do not see our oneness with the earth we don't mind ransacking its resources to live luxuriously. If the rest of creation is separate from us then we fear it more and are more inclined to subdue, control, and exploit it. If being human means being in partnership with creation, we cease to be fully human when we reduce the humanity of another person or we elevate our species above the rest of the universe. To be human is to be free and just and to be a partner of creation: creation's advocate, not creation's boss.

We can see that there are plenty of reasons to act violently but none of these are healthy or likely to lead to outcomes we want. None of them bring salvation to the world. Deference leads to an externalized morality projected onto the powerful people we seek to please. Fear causes us to operate out of a desire for self-preservation and dislocates us from others.

Helplessness is rooted in our failure to see alternatives to violence, often because violence, of one form or another, is so readily available to us. Our worldview teaches us that justice favors the mighty and dignifies our violence, projecting authority onto might. Scapegoating results from a failure to deal adequately with the sources of conflict among us; it leads to a false and temporary peace and an endless spiral of violence. Inhumanity makes violence a more palatable option because our fear and desire to dominate are partners in making us neurotic and ever more power-hungry as a species.

For each reason to choose violence there is a nonviolent alternative. This option needs to be chosen each moment, and lived in, as we reintegrate with our true humanity. Walter Wink calls this the 'third way' of Jesus: It is the constructive and restorative way of nonviolent resistance that we find in the Bible and most explicitly in the New Testament. Being compassionate is an act of resistance; it is different from being caring, or passive. Compassion, literally meaning 'to suffer with', is rooted in our loving desire to be alongside one another in our common struggle for a better spiritual and social reality. Compassion is an act of resistance because the compassionate cannot rest until all suffering has ended. Compassion is the recognition that none of us are free until we are all free.

Building Compassionate Communities

Suggestions for building a compassionate community of resistance where we are:

For Small Groups

Think of a violent situation and try to identify the sources of violence.

Further Reading

Lisa Isherwood, *Weep Not for Your Children: Essays on Religion and Violence*, Equinox, 2007.

Rene Girard, *I See Satan Fall Like Lightning*, Orbis, 2001.

James Allison, *Living in the End Times: The Last Things Re-Imagined*, SPCK, 1997.

Jacques Semelin, *Unarmed Against Hitler: Civilian Resistance in Europe, 1939–1943*, Praeger, 1993.

Ann Morisy, *Bothered and Bewildered: Enacting Hope in Troubled Times*, Continuum, 2009.

For more information, resources, and a chance to feed back your experiments and ideas, visit: www.compassionistas.net

4

Compassionate Resistance

The existential step that the word nonviolence signals leads out of the forced marriage between violence and cowardice.
Dorothee Soelle

If violence is that which dehumanizes, compassion is that which preserves and promotes human dignity. The response to each of the sources of violence, expanded on above, is found in the compassion modeled by Jesus. Compassionate resistance is that which preserves the dignity of all creation in the face of violent systems.

The principle of compassion as a means of resisting the violence of unjust systems offers a practical response more than a moral standard. Moral dilemmas, after all, are a luxury only those with the space to debate enjoy. Powerless people often are too busy surviving to moralize. The biblical texts, notably in the Psalms and the book of Job, often offer a fairly unique view into the world as seen from the underside of history. The Bible has an incredible way of bringing into conversation, in a single library of texts, both imperial and revolutionary wisdoms. The violent emotional outpourings are not hidden or justified but rather they are laid bare. It is no wonder that those of us from comfortable quiet suburbs often struggle with the violence of the psalmists; we are used to being protected from the wrath of the oppressed and from our own raw desire to punish. We have no right to take the violent option away from the marginalized but nor can we say that it leads to peace and justice. There is another option – compassionate resistance – and it is a practical option.

Compassionate resistance is a compelling force. Conversion of oppressive elite groups may be the hope of those who trust in the work of the Spirit of God. But there is no guarantee that, on seeing the vulnerable humanity of the oppressed, oppressors will repent and change their ways. Compassion is not a way of persuading the powerful to a change of heart but, by forcing the structural realities to align with the compassion of God, it makes dehumanizing options unviable.

Compassion is inclusive, universal, and natural. It does not require good people, but people willing to live and learn from one another. From birth through childhood the human displays a natural ability to oppose the power of the adults with nonviolent resistance. Between them, my young children have already made effective use of the hunger strike, the work-to-rule, the all-out strike, the walk-out, going limp when I want to move them, screaming in order to draw sympathy from others, misdirection, forlornness, the dreaded tantrum and many other tricks. They did not learn these from their nursery school teachers. They just responded, as weaker parties with strong wills, to the daunting will of their parents.

Compassion is universal because it only succeeds when its aim is the liberation of both the oppressor and the oppressed from unjust structures. It is self-regulating because it cannot be used to bring about oppression. Nonviolent resistance keeps our own violence in check. If you can use violence to successfully bring about justice – put down your weapon – you are the oppressor. If you cannot use violence to bring about justice raise up your head – your salvation is at hand.

Compassionate resistance is an untapped resource. In all of modern history we have barely scratched the surface of possibilities. Although we have an innate adeptness when it comes to nonviolent resistance, what we rarely do is refine this skill with study, training, and practice. Universities all over the world study war but few study peace.

It is not in the interests of nation states to encourage the study of nonviolent resistance because it is the activity they fear the most and because they have invested so much, mythically, histor-ically, and economically, in the practices of war. If the citizens of a nation discover the power of nonviolence their first target is never a neighboring state; it is always their own political elite.

We cannot assume that nonviolent means are either slower or faster than violence. We need only compare the sudden overthrow of Ceausescu with the Hundred Years War between France and England to see that while violence can often bring a swift end to conflict there is no guarantee, and while those committed to nonviolence must prepare for the long haul they may sometimes discover a tipping point where their actions deliver sudden and incredible social change.

Compassion demands constant work towards local social cohesion: bringing into community those who are considered suspect or as outsiders. In 1939 at the height of their power, the Third Reich began a secret program of killing and cremating those considered to have incurable mental illness. The operation, often referred to as 'T4', after the main operation headquarters at 4 Tiergartenstrasse, Berlin, was kept secret for fear of public outrage. They particularly feared upset in three arenas: the military (because soldiers know that they are often the ones who end up with mental health problems from war trauma); family and friends of the executed; and the Churches. Initially there was little civilian protest; through disbelief, ignorance, and helplessness people and institutions kept quiet. But eventually the cracks began to show. In the summer of 1941 the Bishop of Munster denounced the 'assassinations' of the mentally ill and called upon all Christians to resist. His words were followed by those of many other bishops and reverberated around both Church and military. One devout Christian and aviator, honored with the Iron Cross, publicly denounced the practice of euthanasia and was arrested. By August of the same year the program of executing those deemed mentally ill was cancelled and never recommenced.

During the rise of Nazism across Europe, it was often those countries where there was genuine integration of Jewish communities with the non-Jewish majority where many Jewish lives were saved, principally through nonviolent resistance. Even in Germany the most effective efforts to save the lives of Jews came through civil disobedience of people-smuggling and even open-air protest. And the Church, so often remembered for complicity with the Nazi Party, successfully intervened in the state-sponsored extermination of people with mental illness. Resistance from within Germany was harder than anywhere else in Europe: the Nazis came to power through legitimated democratic means; the resistance lacked support from abroad and was fractured from within. Nonetheless, far from fighting to end the holocaust Britain was complicit with anti-Jewish propaganda and Churchill was openly racist. Our media at home only revealed the full horrors of the holocaust after the war ended so it was never a motive for fighting against the Nazis.

The reality is that tyrants fear nonviolent resistance far more than tanks and warplanes. In France, and even Germany, pockets of popular protest, even at the height of Hitler's power, forced Nazi climb-downs and saved lives. In Norway and Holland attempts to control public professions by ordering membership of fascist bodies and the exclusion of Jews failed because of mass letter writing, public protest, non-co-operation leading to hard labor and imprisonment, and the garnering of public outrage. Bulgaria and Denmark were both controlled by Nazi officials yet in both countries nearly all Jews were saved by denouncements and threats of direct action from the Church leaders, occupation of public administration buildings, strikes, covert and overt sabotage, mockery, public gatherings and protests, and unions working to rule. All of this was achieved despite the modest amount of training and literature available on nonviolent resistance at the time. Imagine what could be possible if we honed our skills of subversion.

The Third Reich knew what to do with pacifists and with soldiers but Hitler feared nonviolent resistance because it made it impossible for him to carry out a pogrom against Jews, homosexuals, and other minorities and because it made tyranny an outright and ridiculous impossibility. Oppressive forces always have their upper limit of resources after which they rely entirely upon the acquiescence of the oppressed.

But since most nations' governments are not geared up to nonviolent resistance, nor do the nations themselves have the social cohesion that makes such large-scale resistance possible, we default to war. And because humans tend to justify their behavior in hindsight, in order to live with themselves, we call this 'just war' when what we should really call it is a failure to choose compassion over violence.

The Compassion of Jesus

A case can be made for compassion as a practical option but it is also an important biblical tradition, some of which will be explored below. Compassion is inclusive because it chooses to 'suffer with' rather than cause to suffer; it is a compelling force because it goes to the root causes of oppression; it is a mostly untapped resource that requires both training and social cohesion. It forces us to go beyond the jingoism of just war theory to try and find the real causes of war and it is something the powerful simply don't know how to handle. It should not surprise us that Jesus was an exemplar of compassionate resistance; indeed it was central to his mission to restore the compassion of God.

To understand the place of compassion in the activism of those who follow the ways and teachings of Jesus we must have some sense of how Jesus understood it. We will look mostly at Matthew's Jesus and the 'Sermon on the Mount', although Mark, Luke, and to some extent John's gospel all give us a similar pattern of love and resistance to work from.

Jesus' clearest teaching on nonviolent resistance can be found in Matthew's gospel, chapters 5 and 6; often called the Sermon on the Mount. These chapters offer a good lens through which to explore the rest of Jesus' ministry and Paul's letters. For Paul we will turn initially to his letters to the Romans and the Ephesians although when we come to chapter fourteen we will look more broadly at St Paul's propaganda of resistance to empire.

To begin then let's consider a familiar quote from Matthew's Jesus that needs looking at in what might be an unfamiliar way:

But I say to you, do not resist an evildoer. But if anyone strikes you on the right cheek, turn the other also; and if anyone wants to sue you and take your coat, give your cloak as well; and if anyone forces you to go one mile, go also the second mile.
(Matthew 5:38–42)

The translator's version above is doing no worse than basing its reading on the King James or Authorized Version, 'resist not an evildoer', but this translation is biased toward encouraging passivity among the baptized subjects. It was published under a king's patronage, in a time when the feudal social set-up made a great virtue of deference. Tolstoy wrote, and contemporary translators agree, that a better rendering of the Greek word would be 'do not resist evil by force'[7] or 'resist without violence'.

There is a world of a difference between 'do not resist' and 'do not resist violently'. The latter not only does not prohibit resistance but also gives instruction on how to resist appropriately. It is possible – even necessary and practical – according to Matthew's Jesus, to resist violence with nonviolence.

We may think, however, that if Jesus wanted his disciples to use nonviolent resistance he would at least give them some clue as to how. Fortunately Jesus gives more than a hint of both method and reasoning for it. In the passage quoted above, Jesus asks his disciples to do three things: turn the other cheek; give your cloak; walk the extra mile. None of these are straight-forward commands, but rather a blueprint for a new way of thinking. And they need some serious unpacking.

First is turning the other cheek. Popular understanding is that this is about refusing to fight back. 'Just War' theory means this is often softened to not fighting back on your own behalf, but if it can be shown to be motivated by someone else's interest then fighting is okay. Often this motivation is fictional like Iraqi weapons of mass destruction; sometimes it's after the fact like the Holocaust.

In first-century Galilee, were a person to smack a social inferior on the cheek, the superior might use the back of the right hand. The back of the hand denotes superiority and since the left hand is 'unclean', due to its association with wiping your bum, the right hand is the only option. If the victim of the smack were to turn the other cheek, s/he would force the assailant into a dilemma. To smack the other cheek would entail either using the palm – denoting an equality that humiliates the attacker – or using the back of the left hand, thus breaking a taboo that would also humiliate the attacker. If Walter Wink is right, this completely changes the force of the saying. To turn the other cheek is not to give in to violence but to creatively, even mischie-vously, resist it.

Second, Jesus asks his listeners to give up both tunic and cloak. If this is a simple call to Christian charity then all well and good, and as a rich white man I'm inclined to read the saying as though a poor person is asking me for charity and I should give even more. If I were to read it this way it would certainly be resonant with the rest of Jesus' teaching. But there is more to it. And the original audience were probably more accustomed to receiving handouts than giving them.

We know that the only reason to take someone's cloak in first-century Galilee is if they owe you money: the cloak acts as a guarantee of the loan. But if the one needing the loan is homeless, the cloak may be all that separates that person from the cold night. Furthermore, for a first-century Jew to look on another's nakedness was a taboo more shameful than to be naked. When Noah got drunk and took off his clothes it was his son, who saw his naked body, who was shamed.

Jesus' idea is that when a loan shark demands an exploitative mortgage, the debtor should use public scorn of breaking a taboo and vulnerable humanity to shame the powerful lender and lay on social pressure. This must be done as a public act of witness against the powerful. Although the poor person is naked, the lender is exposed as the cause.

Finally, 'going the extra mile' must be considered in the light of the etiquette of Roman occupation. The Romans, like all occupying forces, liked to believe their actions tough but fair. So it was that Roman soldiers were permitted to force a peasant to carry their load for one mile *but not a step further*. And since officers made such a big deal of discipline, the punishment a soldier would receive for breaking the military code would be severe.

Imagine the scene: a peasant is forced to carry a load – perhaps a shield and a bag of equipment. As they pass the way-marker the soldier calls out, 'That's enough, peasant, put it down here; I'll find someone else soon enough … Peasant! … Oy!' I can see the soldier now half jogging after the subversive load-bearer and half looking over his shoulder in panic lest he be caught breaking his own rule.

It may be that the peasant would get a good beating but again, if Walter Wink is right, this rendering of the text changes the meaning of Jesus' words entirely. No longer is it a gentle and vague instruction about going out of your way to help others. Rather it is about using the rules of the oppressor to your own creative advantage when you have little left to fight with.

If we move back in the text a little to the Beatitudes (Matthew

5:2–12) we can see that Jesus has a clear idea of how spirituality and resistance are two sides of the same coin. Dave Andrews has written powerfully on how the Beatitudes present a 'do-able set of realistic ideals that give us a way to engage a world of poverty and violence'.[8] So, to be 'poor in spirit' is to be in solidarity with the poor, and to be merciful means caring personally for those in need rather than paying someone else to. To mourn is to cry out against felt injustice, as we will discover in chapter eleven. To be meek is not to be subservient but to have self-control under pressure of injustice just as Gandhi's followers became model prisoners on his advice: following prison rules where possible and showing courtesy to their jailers. To be pure in heart is to maintain integrity between action and proclamation, which is why activism without spiritual integrity is not enough to sustain a campaigner for long. To be a peacemaker is to find nonviolent ways to resist the violence of oppression by bringing skills and service to places of conflict; we will look at some of these skills later.

Jesus crowns the Beatitudes with the most challenging ethic of all, the inevitable result of nonviolent resistance: 'Blessed are you when people persecute you and revile you.' We know Jesus took this seriously because of his torture and execution on the outskirts of Jerusalem and we know that the early disciples resisted the religious conclusions folk would draw from Jesus' death – that God cursed him – because of their proclamation of his resurrection.

At the heart of the sermon in Matthew's gospel is the principle behind the practical: God has compassion for everyone, indiscriminately; we should do the same.

> You have heard that it was said, 'You shall love your neighbor and hate your enemy.' But I say to you, Love your enemies and pray for those who persecute you, so that you may be children of your Father in heaven; for he makes his sun rise on the evil

and on the good, and sends rain on the righteous and on the unrighteous. For if you love those who love you, what reward do you have? Do not even the tax-collectors do the same? And if you greet only your brothers and sisters, what more are you doing than others? Do not even the Gentiles do the same? Be perfect, therefore, as your heavenly Father is perfect. (Matthew 5:43–48)

Compassionate resistance is not glamorous and risks misunderstanding, criticism from those we might expect to support us, threats, and imprisonment or execution. It takes the support of a loving and praying community, which is why the first requirement of compassionate activists is always this: get yourself in good company and quick.

Paul and Radical Compassion

Both Jesus and St Paul offer us principles and patterns to help us figure out how and why nonviolent resistance works. These two great figures shaped the early Church. For a long time many people have criticized Paul for diluting Jesus' message. However, more recent studies have uncovered a very different portrait of the saint that locates him more clearly in the Jesus tradition.

Jesus' teaching on loving both friend and foe is unpacked further in Paul's letters written to the churches at Ephesus and Rome. For Paul, loving your neighbor needs to be worked out at every scale of relationship. The letter to the Romans is almost definitely written by the apostle Paul, whereas whoever wrote the letter to the Ephesians was writing some decades later.

The later author was not necessarily trying to deceive people into thinking he was Paul but rather imagining what Paul might have said if he were still around and writing it up as a piece of creative pastoral writing. Both letters tell us about attitudes to violence and resistance to the powers fairly early on in Christian history.

Ephesians gives us the image of a battle that is not physical but neither is it entirely spiritual:

> For our struggle is not against enemies of blood and flesh, but against the rulers, against the authorities, against the cosmic powers of this present darkness, against the spiritual forces of evil in the heavenly places.
> (Ephesians 6:12)

We could interpret this text somewhat fatalistically: Since our struggle is not against flesh and blood, why should we concern ourselves with political matters? But we know that this was not characteristic of Paul and the early Church, which was heavily persecuted for refusing to worship political leaders and for organizing anti-apartheid communities of common purse. Paul also preached a message that confronted the Pax Romana of slavery and submission. The rest of the letter to the Ephesians explains how Christians can be agents of change in harsh political realities.

The author knows that change must be total, systemic, and philosophical, rather than a simple changing of the guard. A military revolution – a struggle with flesh and blood – is never more than a palace coup. One ruler replaces another and has to maintain rule through violence.

The author of the letter to the Ephesians urges his readers and listeners to put on God's armor in a passage that reads like a restyled version of the Beatitudes.

> Put on the whole armor of God, so that you may be able to stand against the wiles of the devil. For our struggle is not against enemies of blood and flesh, but against the rulers, against the authorities, against the cosmic powers of this present darkness, against the spiritual forces of evil in the heavenly places. Therefore take up the whole armor of God, so

that you may be able to withstand on that evil day, and
having done everything, to stand firm. Stand therefore, and
fasten the belt of truth around your waist, and put on the
breastplate of righteousness. As shoes for your feet put on
whatever will make you ready to proclaim the gospel of
peace. With all of these, take the shield of faith, with which
you will be able to quench all the flaming arrows of the evil
one. Take the helmet of salvation, and the sword of the Spirit,
which is the word of God.
(Ephesians 6:11–17)

Truth, righteousness, proclamation of peace, faith, salvation, and
the sword of the spirit are all weapons of the compassion of
Jesus.

But it is with the early letters of Paul where we find the
clearest primitive commentary on the Sermon on the Mount.
Ironically we find it in the very passage of scripture that is most
readily used to advocate subservience to unjust powers: Romans
chapters 12 and 13. The letter to the Romans is probably the last
of the letters written by St Paul; as such Romans represents a
culmination of ten years of Jesus-oriented compassionate
activism.

The letter is as dense as it is long, with themes of salvation,
love, and a refusal to be conformed to 'this age'. When Jesus, or
Paul, refers to 'this age' or 'the world', they are not addressing
the physics of space and time but the social, political, and philosophical reality that encompasses and overwhelms ordinary
people: the systems.

I want to pause a moment to address a challenge I have heard
over and again in relation to St Paul: But what about Romans 13?

Let every person be subject to the governing authorities; for
there is no authority except from God, and those authorities
that exist have been instituted by God. Therefore whoever

resists authority resists what God has appointed, and those who resist will incur judgment. For rulers are not a terror to good conduct, but to bad. Do you wish to have no fear of the authority? Then do what is good, and you will receive its approval; for it is God's servant for your good. But if you do what is wrong, you should be afraid, for the authority does not bear the sword in vain!
(Romans 13:1–4)

Romans chapter 13 has been used by generations of leaders and politically passive Christians to justify acquiescence to oppression. It is usually the same people who justify war by reference to Hitler, conveniently ignoring this text and finding some other proof-text to argue from.

The problem is they are reading Romans 13 as though it is separate from chapter 12. In fact chapters 12 and 13 are a single unit of argument for indiscriminate compassion. Paul begins this unit by calling for the saints in Rome to 'let love be genuine' (12:9) by honoring and offering material support (vv. 10–12). This is love within the community and is difficult to argue against. But Paul goes on to instruct, 'Bless those who persecute you' (v. 14) and 'associate with the lowly' (v. 16), and 'If your enemies are hungry, feed them' (v. 20).

Like Jesus, Paul realizes that the real enemy is the system and that surviving within an unjust system while covertly undermining it is no easy task. Like Jesus he makes loving even the enemy the key principle of resistance while cautioning against the type of resistance that typified the communal riots that had led to the exile of most Jews living in Rome around that time.

Paul offers his advice on handling the Roman Empire in a way that acts as a commentary on Jesus' invitation to love our enemies. Although Paul seems to be urging compliance with the Romans when he writes that they are 'the servant of God to execute wrath on the wrongdoer' (Romans 13:5), he is really trying to help his readers understand love of enemy in the face of state terror. Remember Paul was beaten, transported, near-drowned, and placed under house arrest by the Roman Empire.

Paul has seen crucifixion and execution of Jews and non-Jewish followers of Jesus so he is not naïve about the evil done in the name of divine authority. However, he also knows that resistance to evil must be pure in intention and perfect in love and so advocates an approach to empire that acts with restraint, treats the enemy with respect, and loves entirely.

Paul encourages the early Christian communities to 'let love be genuine', 'love one another', 'bless those who persecute', aim to 'live peaceably with all', 'overcome evil with good' (all in Romans 12). It is in this context that he calls for submission to authority, not because the actions of authority figures are valid but because it is only through loving and patient resistance that evil will be overcome.

We will return to Paul in our chapter on methods of shalom resistance as we start to discover a very different profile of this saint, from the Paul earlier generations have handed on to us. For now we can see that both Jesus and Paul, far from being mild-mannered conformists, offer a radical model of love and peace that offers a practical alternative to the loyalty and pacification required by empire. Jesus' Sermon on the Mount is a political manifesto for those at the brutal end of empire's ambitions. Paul offers a pragmatic model for alternative communities struggling to survive at the heart of empire. Both Paul and Jesus offer a third way between violence and domestication: nonviolent loving resistance that is personally and socially transforming.

It is important to look broadly: at systems, trends, and institutions, in order to understand what tactics and strategies to use to bring about real change. But it is no less important to understand that all real change happens only at a personal level. Anything that looks at the big picture is only important as far as it affects our decisions and actions in the communities where we live and work. This is the essence of personalism: making relationships personal, and taking personal responsibility for the wellbeing of the real people we meet as we go about our lives. In the next chapter we will look at how what we do – our labor – and how we respond to suffering – justice – must always be personal, and discover that in understanding and living the change we want to see in the world we learn what changes are necessary. We can read as many books and have as many ideas as we like but only in our own experiments can we understand both the symptoms and the roots of suffering in our societies. Compassion is always personal.

Building Compassionate Communities

Suggestions for building a compassionate community of resistance where we are:

For Small Groups

Identify someone, or an organization, harming your community. Consider how they might want you to pray and then commit yourselves to pray regularly for their welfare.

Further Reading

Dave Andrews, *Plan Be: Be the Change You Want to See in the World*, Authentic, 2009.

Walter Wink, *Jesus and Nonviolence: A Third Way*, Fortress, 2003.

Marcus J. Borg and John Dominic Crossan, *The First Paul: Reclaiming the Radical Visionary behind the Church's Conservative Icon*, SPCK, 2009.

For more information, resources, and a chance to feed back your experiments and ideas, visit: www.compassionistas.net

5

Making Community Personal

To exist free of violence means ... to think and act with other living beings in common life.
Dorothee Soelle

In the previous chapter we looked at the way Jesus' and St Paul's teachings and actions reflected their radical compassion for people. Both biblical characters were deeply concerned with the people they lived among as well as the dominating systems that caused those people to suffer. Because their compassion was always personal so was their assessment of the systems of injustice.

I don't know how many conversations I have that include phrases like these but more than anyone needs to:

- 'So I had to say "no" to the grant because we just couldn't do that.'
- 'It can't be pizza; the money comes from a "healthy eating" grant.'
- 'I've just been awarded £2000; we've got to use it by next month on getting single mothers to improve their literacy.'
- 'If we're going to tick the boxes then we're going to forget the people it's for.'

Personalism, put simply, is the expectation that we take responsibility for the wellbeing of all with whom we meet. We do not contract out the love and care we should show to those in need to professional carers when we can well meet that need among ourselves. We do not find external funding to cover the cost of compassion so that our personal finances remain untouched by the reality of the marginalized. Personalism is the desire to be transformed by the person we encounter in our life journey so that both they and we are richer for the encounter.

The long-term pursuit of compassionate activists is the skilling-up of individuals and communities in personal and social healing stories and techniques. Authentically following the example of Jesus means recognizing the importance of the person in front of me. It means recognizing my spiritual connection to that person and our shared connection with the divine spark in all of us.

Individualism and personalism are opposing approaches to our social crisis. Individualism feeds the capitalist model where everything, including compassion, can be bought and sold. The individual strives to be materially and emotionally self-sustaining while becoming increasingly dependent on a system beyond individual control.

Personalism assumes that we have collective needs and an ability to express a consensus and that this can only be done as we learn to meet one another with personal responsibility. Individualism makes the needs of others less important than our own needs and manufactured wants. Personalism seeks to hear the needs of others and find ways to communicate our own real needs.

Mercy Is Always Personal

The Catholic Worker model is one of the Houses of Hospitality. Catholic Workers are usually committed to showing compassion on a personal level and primarily in the context of a safe and hospitable space like around the table or in a shared house.

The Catholic Worker movement began in New York in the 1930s with the work of Dorothy Day, Peter Maurin, and their friends. They opened up ordinary homes, without recourse to grants or wealthy patrons, to the homeless and destitute. Often they lived off whatever they could beg from others and by sharing broadly they were able to meet all their needs and live generously.

Today Catholic Workers around the world find new and traditional ways of expressing what Day and others lived. The London Catholic Workers are based around four houses: three of these houses have members of the community and guests living together and the fourth has been given over entirely to asylum seekers while the rent is found each month by community members living elsewhere.

From these community houses many activities are resourced including a cafe, discussion groups, agricultural projects, parties, and active war resistance. If members are sent to prison for challenging military powers the rest of the community is there prayerfully, emotionally, and materially to support them. Furthermore, being community intentionally draws others into the edges of community life. Compassionate activism and commitment to shared life are integral to one another.

If we first examine needs as personal we begin by thinking about how we communicate our real needs to ourselves. Most of the time, if we're honest, we do this badly and when we feel hurt or threatened we get even further off the mark.

A few months ago I was driving along the motorway; my wife was in the passenger seat and our two young children in the rear. As I began to pull onto a slip road someone driving at an incredible speed overtook me on the inside and only avoided disaster because I responded by slowing down. As we pulled up behind the car at the roundabout I turned to my wife.

'Right now I'm imagining getting out of the car, going over to that bloke's car, opening the door, dragging him out and giving him the beating of his life.'

My wife pointed out two important things. First, that does not sound very compassionate and second, I'm not really much of a fighter. Thanks!

'But what about the Psalms? They're full of violent emotional outpourings. If I want to fantasize about dashing him against the hood that's perfectly reasonable.'

She chose not to pursue the conversation.

But as we drove out onto the A-road I remembered what I had been reading recently about compassionate communication.[9] I examined my anger more closely and asked myself what basic needs were not being met because of this stranger's actions. I need to feel safe; I need to feel that I can keep the people in this car safe.

My anger concealed my childlike fear of death. Also, the shock the stranger gave me created an outlet for other frustrations in my own life; his actions gave other sources of anger a convenient outlet. I wondered about the frustrations in the other driver's life and whether the car was the only place he felt in control. Certainly that's what the car adverts promise us, among other things. By now my anger had given way entirely to a more meaningful, honest, array of thoughts and emotions and recognized needs.

Jesus often asked of people, 'What do you really need?' or 'What do you want from me?' Otherwise he himself would direct them to their more basic desires, needs, and false perspectives, helping them to work these things out for themselves through a story that reflects their reality back at them but with a twist, as does the story about a Samaritan who helps a badly injured man (Luke 10:25–37). A spirituality of confession, reconciliation, absolution, self-examination such as offered in the breadth of spiritual practices can help both followers of Jesus and those who are just looking for the right tools for the job, to reshape their character in relation to an otherwise seemingly hostile world.

Just as Jesus ministered within a community, so community discernment and consensus is vital to any compassionate activism. Community is a place of encouragement, accountability, character-forming worship, and intentionality. Community comes in many forms: a local church, an extended household with some sort of common purse and collective vocation, an affinity group and so on.

Affinity groups are often temporary and always small groups with the shared intention of addressing a particular social injustice. It is recommended that the group share more in common than the particular issue around which they are gathering; they might have a religious perspective in common, or they might all like *Doctor Who* – whatever it is it provides another level of affinity that strengthens the group. When involved in blockading a site involved in violence and/or injustice, several affinity groups working on separate but agreed aspects of the direct action help to decentralize the decision-making while keeping the flow of information to a necessary minimum. This keeps the covert nature of a direct action both efficient and secure. Within such a group there are temporary defined roles – some might be willing to be arrested if necessary, others to be legal observers, others still to offer support, creativity, and whatever needs are agreed.

The most straightforward way of bringing personal and inter-personal transformation is through acts of mercy. We have already looked briefly at the Catholic Worker model to which the 'works of mercy' are integral. Catholic Workers often have open tables for food and fellowship and will deliberately put their own bodies in the way on behalf of the innocent facing the violence of the state or imprisonment, in order to protect the most vulnerable.

Matthew's gospel has Jesus presenting an apocalyptic vision in which the 'Son of Humanity' or 'King' returns at the end of time to judge between those who talk the talk and those who walk the walk. He separates them into those who helped him and those who didn't.

Then the righteous will answer him, 'Lord, when was it that we saw you hungry and gave you food, or thirsty and gave

you something to drink? And when was it that we saw you a stranger and welcomed you, or naked and gave you clothing? And when was it that we saw you sick or in prison and visited you?' And the king will answer them, 'Truly I tell you, just as you did it to one of the least of these who are members of my family, you did it to me.'
(Matthew 25:37–40)

In the parable of the sheep and the goats we are reminded that when we clothe the naked, visit the prisoner, feed the hungry, shelter the homeless, and visit the lonely we are doing these things for Jesus. Jesus is the schema for victims who refuse to be scapegoats and steam valves for unjust systems. Jesus' death was supposed to signal his guilt for the unjust system he lived in but instead the disciples made it clear that God did not approve the death of Jesus or the system of scapegoating the innocent.

Each time we commit ourselves to an act of mercy toward the victims of our system, we declaim our system in the very act of care. We have an ugly saying in Britain: 'the undeserving poor'. These are people who are not only considered to be blamed for their own plight but they are what is wrong with society generally: in the past this has often been Jews but today it is single mums, people who use illegal drugs, Muslims, people on benefits. Caring for them, we are told, encourages them in the behaviors that destroy the fabric of society.

Meaningful Labor Is Always Personal

If alienation from the earth, and from our own bodies, is endemic in a fractured society, meaningful labor is essential to our salvation. A return to the work of our hands in the messiness and goodness of creation reacquaints us with that which terrifies us – the wilderness.

Labor brings us into greater solidarity with those for whom it is not an option but a necessity; it allows us to learn the spiritual discipline of being fully present to the moment. The greater our dependence on technological society, the more wistful and unsatisfying our activity is. The very practice of giving ourselves entirely to the task in hand challenges the powers because it leaves no space for their worship or values to hold us down.

St Benedict wrote, 'The one who labors as they pray lifts their heart to God with their hands.' Meaningful labor re-orients us spiritually as well as physically toward both God and the universe. It is a state of rest in itself and, because meaningful labor is just, its result is a state of rest too.

Just as labor defies the powers so too does the practical wisdom of Sabbath-keeping. To keep the Sabbath means to rest, but only in a very particular context. Jesus' words that 'the Sabbath is for people, not people for the Sabbath' remind us that the practice of Sabbath-keeping is neither legalistic nor moral but practical in intention. To keep the Sabbath in the broadest sense is to have completed the task of creation, to find a world in balance, harmony, and healed. But our regular practice of rest allows us to prefigure that in our lives.

The Sabbath is for our selves, for the land, and for our wallets. By resting ourselves we give space for God's work in us and for our own enjoyment of all that already is; it reminds us that we are not essential to the work of salvation – the world still spins even as we rest.

The Sabbath is for the land because to always be looking for its productivity instead of allowing nature to takes its own space and pace is too dominating. In recent Christian history we have tended to speak of God and creation in a way that justifies human domination of nature. Yet when we compare the places where humans have most dominated nature to where we have interfered the least, the argument for benign human rule of nature becomes impossible to maintain.

Finally the Sabbath is for our wallets. We blaspheme the Money God every time we make a choice not to spend or accumulate wealth, every time we see its use as a means rather than an emotional end in itself, and every time we choose to find ways to interact and thrive in our community without reference to money.

The biblical Sabbath is woven in with the idea of Jubilee economics: the principle that since all belongs to God, exploitation of the land for profit defies God's story. Debts must be regularly cancelled and slaves freed of all obligations and made full citizens again so that social cohesion and healing can return.

Justice Is Always Personal

Personal healing includes person-to-person healing. This is an endless revolution since every interaction brings with it the risks of wounding, jealousy, and competition.

We have already begun to explore nonviolent communication as defined by Marshall Rosenberg. There are places around the world where this method is taught and worked out in detailed practice but the basic four steps of the process are easily summarized. Rosenberg encourages us to identify:

1 The concrete actions we observe that affect our wellbeing.
2 How we feel in relation to what we observe.
3 The needs, values, desires, and so on that create our feelings.
4 The concrete actions we request in order to enrich our lives.

When we encounter a position or action taken by another person that creates a violent reaction in ourselves, most of us turn into one of the following: a hedgehog, a teddy bear or a rhinoceros. Which one we are depends in part on our habit and in part on the person who has annoyed us. Hedgehogs curl up into a prickly ball; they sulk and prickle – we know we've upset them but it is difficult to communicate directly with them. Teddy bears just give in to the desires of the other person even to their own detriment; this manages the conflict okay unless someone else is getting hurt, which puts the teddy bear in something of a dilemma. Rhinoceroses pride themselves on their ability to say exactly what they mean and if people don't like it that's their problem. Rhinos charge in, all emotions blazing, in a confrontation, determined not to be put upon and only superficially understanding what the conflict is about.

The four-step process outlined above takes careful questioning of both the self and the other. It involves a feedback loop of listening and clarifying the value-judgment statements in order to get to the real needs that lie beneath them.

Compassionate communication assumes that the initial aggressive statement or action is not at the heart of the matter but a signpost along the way. Careful reading of the map of conversation has the assumption that, however unpleasantly we experience the expressions of the other, there is a human need wanting to be met at the bottom of it. We live in a world where we rarely properly listen to one another, preferring rather to queue politely for our turn to speak, nodding agreeably as we do so. But we each need to be honored with being properly heard.

Forgiveness is always personal but finding a way for any victim of injustice to forgive an offender is often challenging. We have been taught to believe that the natural human response to being offended against is to seek retribution. If this is true then the role of the state penal system is to curb our desire to inflict violence on one another. There is an assumption in the state penal system that justice is found in retribution rather than reconciliation, an assumption that is not borne out by the experience of those who work to bring victims and offenders together.

Restorative Justice (RJ) is a process of bringing victims and offenders together in a space in order to hear one another's story and respond to one another's real un-met needs. RJ is often used among prisoners but can be found in communities and institutions too. It is an increasingly popular tool for bringing together those we call 'offenders' and 'victims' with a third party in order to facilitate restitution rather than punishment.

In the UK justice being done is usually understood in terms of 'penal justice'. We see victims of crime through the news media telling us how angry they are because the offender has been given too short a sentence. Through bitter tears they tell us that justice has not been done. This does not mean that their instinctive response is punishment of the offender but it shows how totally we have taken on board this way of thinking.

RJ allows the victim or victims to speak clearly of the way they have been harmed in as complete a way as they can manage. They do so without interruption from the offender. It is good practice for the offender to have told the story from their point of view beforehand to a third party and to have shown awareness that what they did was their responsibility and that it caused harm. Only in hearing the victim directly and completely, the offender begins to understand the consequences of violent actions.

An example recently and close to where I live was of a burglary. The burglar had nearly served his sentence when the RJ process began. When he sat down in front of one of the victims, he discovered that he had robbed the house of a young couple who were trying for their second child. The female partner had been in the house at the time of the burglary and became so anxious about not feeling safe that conception of the second child was delayed for over a year. Meanwhile the first child was scared to return to her room where items were stolen. The burglar showed shock and remorse but was then allowed to share his story of single-parent struggle and drug addiction. The victim was asked to suggest a means of restoration.

What is fascinating about the next step is that the victim's instinct was not for humiliation or punishment. Instead it was for the offender to write a letter to his daughter apologizing and promising never to return to the house, to enter a drug rehabilitation program, and to get in a better financial position to care for his own child. The offender agreed to do these things and the victim was keen to be kept up to date on progress on all of the requirements.

There is huge scope for those engaged in compassionate communication to get trained in RJ and make themselves available to their communities both to facilitate it and to teach the skills required for when a third party is not needed. In all personal offender–victim situations there is a context whereby the powers are exerting pressures that lead to conflicts. By healing and equipping to heal in these instances, compassionate activism helps us to identify ways in which the powers have taken control over aspects of our lives and to begin to wrestle with these angels and demons to gain greater liberty and humanity.

Personal Is Always Structural

A commitment to transforming personal relationships instead of individual lives creates the necessary space for love, mercy and the authentic meeting of one another's needs. Personalism challenges the logic of penal justice by offering a more human response to conflict. It challenges us to have a more meaningful relationship with our work. Personalism requires us to show mercy rather than pay others to show mercy on our behalf and so causes us to confront our own culpability in the systems that lead to the world of un-met needs.

Compassionate activists cannot truly understand the system they wish to change without personally knowing those who suffer most because of it. Giving and receiving hospitality is always the first step to analyzing the powers. It is little use and sometimes unhelpful to go on marches 'on behalf of' people whom we have not encountered personally through listening to their stories.

South American 'base communities' encourage us to read the Bible from the point of view of those on the margins of society, indeed to read society through the eyes of the oppressed with all the social and imaginative tools available to us. To be poor in spirit, or spiritually poor, is to be in concrete solidarity with poor communities and to be changed both inwardly and behaviorally by these encounters. This allows us to examine ourselves and be converted evermore clearly to the gospel of the poor and to discover our motives, aims, and the stories that shape our decisions.

Compassionate activists must seek authentic personal solidarity with marginalized people. Only then can any analysis of the powers and engagement with the powers be possible. This is not a straightforward task; those who are most oppressed are often made conservative by their oppression. If your life is lived on a knife-edge, you may be as likely to risk all, as you are to risk nothing on the dim hope of change.

Those who are oppressed the most materially are often equally oppressed in their imaginations; it is as though the oppressor has made a nest in the people's minds and is feathering it with fatalism, conservatism, and low self-esteem. Wealthy folk are converted to the needs of poor communities *through* community and liberationist thinking and acting, but so too are the poor themselves.

Replacing alienating, dehumanizing and pacifying structures of aid with personal mutual help is a hugely important tool transforming communities from individualism, which is vulnerable to the viral messages of the system, to mutual aid that discovers ways to shape futures.

Building Compassionate Communities

Suggestions for building a compassionate community of resistance where we are:

For Small Groups

See how many times in a week you can speak to someone where you might normally send them an electronic message. Journal the experience and share it with someone.

Further Reading

Dorothy Day, *The Long Loneliness: An Autobiography*, Harper and Row, 1952.

Robert Ellsberg (ed.), *Dorothy Day: Selected Writings*, DLT, 2005.

Jonathan Bartley, *The Subversive Manifesto: Lifting the Lid on God's Political Agenda*, BRF, 2003.

For more information, resources, and a chance to feed back your experiments and ideas, visit: www.compassionistas.net

6

Good Shepherds of Community

Community is the place where in togetherness a ladder is built and divine sparks are fashioned and become visible.
Dorothee Soelle

The prophetic tradition of describing rulers as good or bad shepherds was a theme that the Jesus of John's gospel really warmed too. He contrasted good shepherds with 'hired hands'. The good shepherd knew the sheep and was known by the sheep. Good shepherds are leaders from among, not rulers from above.

> I am the good shepherd. The good shepherd lays down his life for the sheep. The hired hand, who is not the shepherd and does not own the sheep, sees the wolf coming and leaves the sheep and runs away – and the wolf snatches them and scatters them. The hired hand runs away because a hired hand does not care for the sheep. I am the good shepherd. I know my own and my own know me, just as the Father knows me and I know the Father. And I lay down my life for the sheep. (John 10:11–15)

Following this model, Jesus' leadership emerged from among those on the margins and he remained part of their community. He cared for the one sheep in a hundred who was found lost and outside the fold.

The hired hands were the client kings of empire, those who are sent in by others to rule primarily for the benefit of imperial bosses. Rulers do not care about the lost sheep at all. In fact, the loss of the occasional sheep is necessary to the process of oppression and control because it scares all the other sheep into submission or provides a suitable outsider on which to blame social unrest.

Bringing the sheep back into the fold is integral to activism because unjust systems require people to be excluded in order to turn them into sacrificial victims at the altar of good order. In other words, as oppressed and chaotic communities, isolated and turned inward, begin to voice their frustration with their material and social circumstances, they look for someone to blame. Because internal conflict is rarely dealt with directly, someone outside the community can be blamed and punished vicariously for the un-dealt-with sin caused by the system.

Every society has people on the margins; as one group finds its voice and integration so another is shunted into the shadows: single mothers, queer folk, black people, Jewish communities, religious minorities, Dalits, communists, and chavs have all taken their turn and continue to do so. Most of the time, these marginal groups are simply kept down and out by the messengers of our age and the powers they represent. Their exclusion is vital to the continued vitality of unjust structures. Because injustice produces social competition and unrest, societies that are not ready to address the true causes of their imbalances must find a surrogate cause. Here the marginal groups take center stage.

Marginal groups act as sacrifices – prepared and offered for the sins of society. When the sacrifice is made there is usually a huge and sudden bloodletting. This was the case with the Jewish holocaust, for example. This bloodletting restores a sense of false peace to society and unites all others in common cause. In the 1930s a humiliated and divide Germany was able to build unity and gain self-esteem through the extermination of Jews, homosexuals, and other minorities.

Ironically the Jewish and Christian communities are the only ones that present this false peace for what it really is through the stories they tell. Job, the prophets, the psalmists, and the gospels all take the voice of the innocent victim and denounce the process of scapegoating. Jesus' resurrection as the innocent 'Human One' defied the political-religious language of scapegoating. The disciples, after Jesus' death, continued to denounce Jesus' execution as a misdirected act based in the myth of redemptive violence.

Those countries that most effectively resisted violence to Jews were hugely aided by the degree of social cohesion and integration of Jews that equipped them to work together against fascism. Identifying, and identifying with, the marginalized is a long-term and vital role of compassionate activists in thwarting the system in its attempt to pass the buck for its sins onto others.

The habit of naming the systems bodily, and imaginatively, is not part of most people's spiritual literacy. We either trust the systems in place or their all-pervasive efficiency renders them invisible. So when things go wrong we don't know whom to blame. We find an outsider to blame, and doing so suits those who have the greatest stake in maintaining business as usual. A lost sheep or two, outside the fold, unprotected and no longer considered 'one of us', serves the purpose.

The pushing of people to the edges of communities needs active resistance. However, if we stop at practical care we are in danger of being steam valves for an unjust system. If we see someone drowning in a river it is not enough to throw him or her a float; we need to pull them back ashore and then head upstream to find out who pushed them in.

The Lost Sheep of Islamophobia

'I have sheep who are not of this fold,' Jesus went on to say. Jesus recognized that the boundaries between them and us were keeping us from acting in solidarity with one another in the face of exploitation. Explicitly drawing in others into relationship without negating their distinctiveness is a pressing task at a time when all over Europe nationalism and violent rhetoric is on the increase.

We are encouraged by both scholarly press and popular media to see two global polarities, with Islam on one side and 'the West' on the other. Muslims in Europe today are treated in much the same way as Roman Catholics were treated at times in post-Reformation Britain. They are symbols of a hostile outside world that challenges supposedly shared ideals.

It was in a large Anglican church in the evangelical tradition where I first experienced the effect of this on a mainstream community group. It was a Sunday congregation of around four hundred mostly affluent families and students. The worship leader encouraged us to 'pray for the city' and people began to call out their prayers. I was horrified but not hugely surprised to hear this prayer: 'Lord, we just pray for the salvation of our city, where the cancer of Islam is spreading all around us.' The demonizing of Islam had become acceptable in 'polite company'.

Leicester was the first English city to have a majority minority population and relations were generally good. I had lived in the heart of the Muslim-majority parts of the city for some time, taught Islam in a local school, and was involved in regular Muslim–Christian dialogue groups so you can imagine how I felt about that prayer. On a national level Muslims are increasingly stereotyped and marginalized, and even the more liberal media tend to focus on negative stories about Muslims. Politicians and religious leaders are vocal in their denunciations of Muslim extremism as though it were an endemic and isolated movement that had nothing to do with the cultural and economic funda-mentalism of western powers.

When I heard a congregation member calling Islam a cancer it reminded me that Muslim–Christian dialogue needed to be expanded from small groups of liberal religious leaders to touch the lives of conservative Christians too. A group of us, including the rector, set to work on forming two groups – one for men and one for women that centered around a meal, a presentation (alternating between people from either religion), and informal discussion.

First we had a meeting of other members of the church to talk about cross-cultural encounters and I went with the rector to one of the mosques I liked to visit regularly. Some of the Christians were initially motivated only by a desire to convert the Muslims to Christianity. However, as the weeks unfolded, the friendship and joy of the men's group grew at an incredible pace and motivations altered equally rapidly. This quickly affected the angel of the church itself.

Leicester has a history of actively celebrating cultural diversity, alongside the usual tensions and chauvinisms. Local community leaders have played an important part in that. But interfaith conversations happen more often, and with greater impact, on the informal scale of everyday life. When we started two Muslim–Christian groups with an evangelical church, the one for men flew and continued for many years while the one organized by and for women did not experience the same success.

Women in Leicester, and other culturally diverse cities, have been engaged in interfaith conversation long before old men formalized it for themselves. In the midst of their invisibility and the struggle women of different faiths are already knee-deep in each other's political, spiritual, and cultural lives. Where they have created those spaces they are the compassionate activists of their communities.

In the summer of 2011 the media spotlight turned to the massacre of young political activists by a right-wing Christian extremist. Anders Behring Breivik was motivated largely by his fear and hatred of Islam as his website and videos explained. He was in regular contact with the English Defence League, a group whose supporters are notorious in Britain for instigating violence against Muslims. When the BBC first presented the news of the bombing and massacre of Oslo, they made it clear that they knew quickly that the lone terrorist was a Norwegian-speaking Scandinavian with connections to the far right and that he was white. So they got the facts straight. Yet almost all of their initial analysis suggested strongly that the attack was as likely to be perpetrated by Muslim fundamentalists as by any other group. They told us it was almost certainly a domestic issue but went on to only interview the Norwegian *foreign* secretary, further framing the story in anti-Muslim propaganda.

The front page of *The Sun* newspaper contained a self-evident lie: that the attack was a jihadist terror attack, and the *Guardian*, a liberal broadsheet, didn't look much better. It is horrifying to acknowledge but the attitude of Breivik and that of most mainstream media are different only by degrees. There is no difference in the end result – the violent scapegoating of those pushed to the edges of empire.

The Lost Sheep of Forgotten People

In the present economic crisis, despite the prime minister's declaration that 'we're all in this together', it has been the poorest communities that have borne the brunt of cuts in public spending. There are people who, because they have no real representation in public life, are forgotten communities. What happens to these communities is that both fatalism and fundamentalism build into extremism, and self-harm.

Many public servants have been made unemployed as their work becomes voluntary or handed over to profit-focused businesses. Many public services have been forced into closure. All this to bail out a failed banking system so that it might continue to generate more wealth and power for the few at the expense of the many.

In my own community of Matson the initial effects of government savings were many. Legal Aid in Britain has been cut and the rules have changed, making it more risky for individuals to challenge corporations, thus in many cases making justice a privilege rather than a right. Youth projects were closed; those who needed professional care, because capitalism had eroded personal responsibility, found they were isolated. Public services like libraries were targeted for closure in mostly the poorest of communities. These communities were deemed unworthy of a library because of lack of use. No attention was paid to the way libraries were set up without reference to the real needs of those communities in the first place.

The library had been around nearly as long as this fifties-built social housing estate and was one of few facilities available to residents. Old people who had once taken their children there turned up one evening as did teenagers, young families, local councilors, and a former MP. Among these people, as we gathered around a six-foot wooden cross, most had little or no connection with organized religion. We had attached books to the cross as a sign of the way the county council were crucifying public service – scapegoating vulnerable services at the altar of an unjust system. Suddenly the Jesus-story was relevant to everyone.

People turned up with clinking bags full of candles in jars that spread out around the cross; a pool of defiant lights. Then we named the powers and their injustice and sang together our own version of a Negro spiritual: 'Were you there when they crucified our library?' Speeches and stillness followed. The headlines that shamed the powerful and the broken system they represent came the next day.

Those of us with the story in our hearts, because we tell it week-by-week and year-by-year, have the gift of recasting it for the stories our communities tell in their struggles today. And if we come from a richly performative community of worship we can also offer energizing, profound, and community-gathering liturgies to help retell those stories in powerful ways.

As a result of this action the MP 'had words' with my Bishop, a Zionist Christian wrote to the Bishop saying, 'If you don't deal with him I will', and in a private meeting with local community leaders a week later, leading councilors and civil servants confessed to being very nervous about getting it wrong again.

At the time of writing the library is not yet safe but the county council have been found to have acted unlawfully in targeting communities like ours and forced into a rethink. Perhaps more importantly, an act of resistance, lamentation, and community-building has taken place that names and exposes both the powers and the scapegoating mechanism they rely on.

The Lost Shepherds

Ann Morisy, community theologian, speaks and writes of the processes of 're-neighboring' and giving people 'story-rich lives'. She tells the wonderful story of a church hall, worn out and unloved, that opened its doors at night to the street homeless. Young people, otherwise trapped in the rat race of work and consumerism, were roped in to sleep over with the guests, often staying for breakfast with them. Old ladies in the congregation cooked the breakfasts or organized the bedding. Others helped people with their legal status or with work or long-term housing. Still others were called in to improve the fabric of the now much-cherished but welcoming building.

Suddenly people had a story to tell and it was both rich and inclusive; the word 'we' became more common than 'I' and it was associated with actions more than opinions. The revolutionary value of radical hospitality, corporately expressed in common service, cannot be exaggerated. People were discovering that they too could be good shepherds of their communities, offering meaningful care and relationship to one another and to the stranger, the naked, and the hungry. It is common service to the oppressed that should mark out the work of those who follow Jesus. It is not just the lost sheep that we need to rediscover but also the lost shepherds.

Political left and right argue about state-operated public

services on the one hand and corporation-operated private services on the other. Profit-oriented services are capricious and prejudicial: political elites beholden to the profit-oriented companies mismanaging state-governed services. Those who enter caring professions find themselves feeling more like hired hands than good shepherds as the system in which they work coerces them into making bad choices and fulfilling abstract managerial roles.

In reality, grassroots-organized acts of common service, which is what local councils were built on, are what generate and sustain re-neighboring and the sort of social cohesion that can lead to widespread dissent from the all-pervasive authority of the systems.

Compassionate activists must find, create, and enlarge all places of authentic mutual care in order to scupper the powers that steal and destroy from the attempt to find more innocents to sacrifice. Compassionate activism involves searching out the lost, holding the hired hands to account for their neglect, and recognizing the good shepherds in our communities and God's working with and in them. Most of all, it involves bringing lost sheep back into the fold. Compassionate activists are the lost shepherds who are beginning to hear the voice of the good shepherd once again.

Building Compassionate Communities
Suggestions for building a compassionate community of resistance where we are:

For Small Groups
Choose two newspapers and begin to identify the lost sheep in their stories.

Further Reading
Ray Gaston, *A Heart Broken Open: Radical Faith in an Age of Fear,*

Wild Goose, 2009.

Barbara Glasson, *The Exuberant Church: Listening to the Prophetic People of God*, DLT, 2011.

Jonathan Bartley, *Faith and Politics After Christendom: The Church as a Movement for Anarchy*, Authentic, 2006.

For more information, resources, and a chance to feed back your experiments and ideas, visit: www.compassionistas.net

7

Mustard Seeds of Change

However small we judge our own power to be, it is certainly greater than we surmise or are prepared to concede.
Dorothee Soelle

Jesus compared the compassion of God with a mustard seed.

> The kingdom of heaven is like a mustard seed that someone took and sowed in his field; it is the smallest of all the seeds, but when it has grown it is the greatest of shrubs and becomes a tree, so that the birds of the air come and make nests in its branches.
> (Matthew 13:31–32)

Mustard seeds are tiny but in Jesus' parable it is miraculously transformed into a tree. Jesus' image of a tree in which birds make their nests reminded his hearers of the prophecies in which empires are described as trees that provide a home for the birds and shelter for animals (Ezekiel 17:23; Daniel 4:12).

The prophets had named the powers by describing them as sheltering trees but Jesus has challenged the powers by promising the impossible: that the least significant seeds will become the root and blueprint for an alternative to empire, providing a different understanding of peace and security; a different tree to shelter under.

What the parable does not explicitly tell us is what a pernicious weed mustard was considered to be in Jesus' day. No sensible-minded farmer would deliberately sow mustard in the field and risk ruining the crop with this rooting, creeping plant that gets in everything and is impossible to get rid of: a bit like

God's new world.

Writer and activist Colin Ward described a world of freedom and justice as being like seeds beneath the snow of our present society. This metaphor can also be used to describe what Jesus meant by the present and to-be-expected compassion of God. For those who live in the hidden places of our society under the cold dead weight of a technological and capitalist system, change can seem impossible. For those of us who look at a broken world it can seem as bleak and beguiling as a field of snow and ice.

But somewhere underneath a field of snow the seeds of new life lie dormant; waiting. A layer of snow is another way of describing the powers and gives us yet another insight into how we can tackle them. We have two tasks: to thaw out the snow and to nourish the seeds beneath. The snow protects the ground beneath it, insulating it from the cold world above, but also stops the seeds from breaking free and being truly alive. As the sun shines, the time is right for the seeds to push through the thawing cold structure, being nourished by its melting-away process and finding new freedom in its dissolution.

The compassion of God is like seeds beneath the snow and the compassionate activists must find ways to dissolve out the powers and nurture shoots of freedom. In this chapter we need to consider the community-organizing model of bringing about a world of justice and peace.

Getting beneath the Snow

The first task in building a new world in the shell of the old is simply to live out life's experiences getting beneath the cold snow of injustice to find the dormant seeds of change below. Listening to and talking to people with patience and joy, in their everyday world, is the ongoing calling of community organizers.

Radical activist Saul Alinsky pioneered the community-organizing model in the immigrant communities of Chicago's 'Back of the Yards' neighborhood. Alinsky makes an important distinction between 'happenings' and 'experiences'. Happenings are undigested experiences, but for a community organizer the ability to reflect on happenings is what experience is made of.

The story of the Back of the Yards Neighborhood Council (BYNC) has inspired political movements around the world. The Council was formed during the 1930s and 1940s in the ghettos of Chicago, around the same time that Dorothy Day developed the Catholic Worker model in the slums of New York. While Day focused on hospitality and war resistance, Saul Alinsky and Joseph Meegan focused on empowering whole communities to hold political agencies, both locally and globally, to account.

Alinsky has developed a whole philosophy of social change that has been adopted by many people, including those involved in youth work or parish ministry, around the world. Above all, he discovered that there are ways to get disparate local communities – each with their own values and agendas – to work together to challenge the elite and take power back.

In 1996 The East London Community Organization (TELCO) was formed using the same model as BYNC. They describe themselves as diverse and a challenge to power:

> Our leaders are black, brown and white; Asian, West Indian, African, Irish, English. We live in high rise council accommodation and in the semi-detached homes of the middle class suburbs, and in all that there is in between. We are Sikh, Hindu, Muslim, Buddhist, Christian and Secular. We are young and we are old, male and female. We are Tories, Liberal Democrats, Greens and Old and New Labour and those with no affiliation.
>
> We believe in building power that is fundamentally reciprocal, where both parties are influenced by each other and mutual respect develops. The power and influence that we seek is tempered by our religious teachings and moral values and is exercised in the fluid and ever-changing relationship

with our fellow leaders, allies and adversaries. We value and seek to operate in the public sphere. We believe that UK public life should be occupied not just by a few celebrities and politicians – but also by the people themselves seeking a part of the action.[10]

One of their most challenging campaigns has been for a living wage for London workers. The official narrative of our gutter press is that state benefits are too high and discourage feckless poor people from seeking work. The reality is not that benefits are too high but that wages are too low.

Ultimately wages are too low because the people who do the work are not the people who make the decisions, but the legislation and contract changes that TELCO push for encouraged many employers to revise their standards of employment. The campaign grew out of a careful listening and organizing process whereby ideas were generated and discussed until workable solutions emerged.

Ideally, reflective process puts the community organizer in the role of facilitator rather than manager of the campaigning. This empowering reflective process is an important reminder that real and lasting change is about developing skills rather than campaigning on behalf of others. Social change is not something one *does to* people but *creates with* people.

For compassionate activists, reflection is done in the light of scripture and tradition and as community. There is God-talk and there is street-talk; finding God in the street-talk and the street in the God-talk transforms our vision of both God and society with every happening that we allow ourselves to carefully reflect on.

Nurturing Seeds of Change

When I first arrived in Matson, the Matson Forum, an informal and leaderless gathering of community professionals, was mostly middle-class outsiders (me included). This is a common set-up in housing estates. Those few locally grown leaders are either put off by the management culture or are just not invited. But local leaders are the real seeds of change.

Local leaders are almost never recognized outside the community. Community leaders are the women who work between the generations tirelessly supporting neighbors, men who everyone seems to know and to whom they point if something needs to get done or a unifying opinion is sought. Community leaders are rarely the politically ambitious members of the community because their ambition is for their community. Identifying grassroots leadership is a tricky task made all the more difficult by external expectations – especially for those of us with a middle-class model of leadership that uses particular ways of speaking and doing things.

Local leaders are the seeds of change, scattered broadly among the community. They may have leadership roles within particular networks of the community but as they develop in leadership they begin to find their role expands into other people's lives. These leaders can identify for themselves, with encouragement, how the systems operate against them. They then begin to draw others into the urge to transform unjust structures. For the compassionate activist this is when reflective listening becomes most important.

Dave Andrews, part of the 'Waiters Union' in Brisbane, Australia, demonstrates this brilliantly. The Waiters Union is a small group of organizers based among the marginal communities of Brisbane. The Union is a network of compassionate activists inspired by Jesus' teachings and mission to bring about real saving change in their community. None of the projects in Brisbane bear the name 'Waiters Union' since building up an organization is far from their minds.

Having hung out with local people and discovered what change was needed, Dave goes through the long but important process of hearing out how their needs may be met. Some ideas may appear dead-ends but Dave doesn't give way to this dominating instinct. Instead he will use gentle questioning to get groups to think through the consequences of an action before deciding what course of action to follow. When finally the group hit upon an idea that resonates with Jesus' principles and methods of social change, he supports them into realizing their goals.

Elated by the success of their actions in confronting the powers, the next step is to introduce the parallels between what they did and what Jesus has already said or done. Dave notices that 'pretty soon these folks begin to ask me before they decide on an action to help them figure out how Jesus might respond and bringing Jesus' Way into the picture becomes a normal part of the deal'.

Of course working in this way is never easy and it is best to start with easy wins and quick rewards so that the newly allied local resistance groups do not lose heart or faith in their own ability to meet their needs. There is nothing glamorous about this kind of work.

Community organizers can find themselves suspected by everyone, accused publicly of all manner of conspiracy, and personally attacked. In just two years of working in Matson I was libeled in the papers regularly, physically threatened at least three times and attacked twice. Interestingly all this abuse came from people outside the community and from the middle classes but usually within the city. My favorite example, incidentally, was a retired head teacher who wrote in the local newspaper that I should be caned. But more ominously framed threats, particularly if you live as part of a household with children as I do, are not something to be taken lightly.

There are many churches and other Christian activists using this model and it is a model that I have used in my brief years in East London and Gloucester. As a priest in Gloucester I have had the enormous privilege of having the gift of time to be alongside people in community. In an area of mostly social housing, for just over 7,000 people, I was able to identify some of the places where people meet and begin to draw connections between these places.

Waiting with the Seasons

If you're in the same place for long enough you'll be in the right place and time eventually. A commitment to place is essential to the transformation of local communities. The capitalist system relies on a mobile workforce. The increased efficiency of our technologies, but most especially the car, allows companies to demand a greater commitment to paycheque than to place. This freedom to move has paved the way – literally paved the way – to a fragmented society where belonging locally means less than ever. For some of us this is a call to refuse the career ladder; for others it's a call to resist the system that forces us to travel further to find employment, leisure, or community. To work at relationships where we live seems counterintuitive when we can cast a wider net to find people who are so like us that little work is needed.

Many small groups or meeting places were long established but permanently vulnerable to drops in membership and funding: members clubs, a youth center, pubs, children's centers, and a wonderful local library currently fighting an arbitrary council decision to shut the place down. But the longer one lives in an area, the more likely it is that the less obvious places of gathering come to one's attention: outside the chemist in the early morning there is a small community waiting for their methadone; in the post office at certain times and days different groups find one another in a regular pattern of queuing and swapping tales.

As the capitalist system begins to over-reach itself, it has chipped away at the desire of the individual to belong to the group. The less dependent we are on one another for material and social welfare, the more we have to rely on financial securities like longer working weeks, insurance covers, and investments that we know compromise our values but we are afraid to grow old without.

The more we relearn what it means to be committed to one another, really committed, the more we blaspheme the Money God who claims to be able to save us from our fear of a lonely uncared-for future for ourselves and those we love. After the hammering taken by the reputation of unions since the 1980s, membership of all kinds of unions in Britain continues to decline overall. It is almost unheard of for people to 'belong with' a political party and regular church attendance has halved in the last forty years. But it isn't completely bleak: gang membership is on the rise; people still need to be affirmed and to belong. A significant minority of ten- to nineteen-year-olds self-report as being in a gang.

While these statistics might send a chill down your spine what it tells above all is that people long to be in company and that this being in company is often an expression of social unrest. Are these postcode gangs wrong to find security in locality? Is their rage against a constantly shifting reality ill founded? Of course not. They articulate better than any social scientist or economist what is wrong with the powers that rule our lives.

Finding out where people either 'belong' or 'nearly belong' and nurturing meaningful belonging and space of resistance to the encroachment of all that squeezes the joy out of life or pours a listless dissatisfaction and loneliness into our hearts – this is the work of compassionate activism for our time, and it can be done in a million different, simple and gentle ways. No glamour or fuss: just good company.

The churchyard visitors have their own rhythms of the year too. I realized after my first year in Matson that the churchyard bins were overflowing the Monday after Mothering Sunday and Father's Day. Strangers came and waited in a short concentrated span in this wonderful space for similar reasons and with deeply personal stories, but they had not become a community nor did they have dealings with the congregation who worshipped inside the building and helped define the outdoor space. Many, but not all, of these casual visitors knew either me or my colleague but there was potential for community, and priests are all about gathering community.

So the day before Mothering Sunday we simply offered hot chocolate and biscuits and a chance to work on the grounds together, and the day before Father's Day we offered fruit punch and another workday. Immediately a fragile new community was born, one which over the years could develop far beyond the private needs of each person tending a grave to the tender care of the living: both the people who visit and the living earth they attend to.

When I first moved to Matson controversial plans for an 'eco' motorway service area were just beginning to emerge. As part of this proposal Mark Gale, the developer/community worker who envisioned it, wanted to create around three hundred local jobs. He needed a shop front in the center of the estate to help people with training. 'The Gateway' soon became a hub for all kinds of activities: credit union, advocacy, a residents' group, job searches, a platform for local musicians and artists to be celebrated in a fair straightforward way.

It has also been my privilege simply to find a home among the people there, and others valued it too. It became a place where I could hear the voices of local people, some of whom had met and overcome challenging situations, and discover something of the Angel of Matson. Since then Gateway has been both an important source of campaigning enthusiasm and a people who have offered me much spiritual, practical, and emotional care.

In Matson, as in many similar communities, there is a whole generation of emerging community leaders who already discuss heatedly their views about loss and struggle for their neighborhood's future and are offering radical alternatives to middle-class values and have begun to bring that challenge to their councilors and Member of Parliament. There is no such thing as a compassionate activist consultant or a flying organizer. If we want to see transformed communities, we need to get beneath the snows of injustice into places where the sun does not yet shine. We must nurture the seeds of change when and where we find them rather than as and when we choose to cast them. We need to wait with the seasons and allow our hopes and those of our neighbors to grow together.

Building Compassionate Communities

Suggestions for building a compassionate community of resistance where we are:

For Small Groups

Draw or write a profile of a community leader. Share it with a critical friend for feedback. Find out what people in your community think makes a good community leader.

Further Reading

Dave Andrews, *Not Religion, But Love: Practicing a Radical Spirituality of Compassion*, The Pilgrim, 2003.

Ann Morisy, *Beyond the Good Samaritan: Community Ministry and Mission*, Geoffrey Chapman, 2003.

For more information, resources, and a chance to feed back your experiments and ideas, visit: www.compassionistas.net

8

Far from Home

No one can feel at home in a world that has to be bought and used up.
Dorothee Soelle

Jesus tells a story of a father who has two sons. One of them asks for his inheritance from the father in advance, which the father gives him, setting the scene for the rest of the story. The impatient son sets off for the big city, spending all his father's resources until he has nothing, and is thus reduced to degrading work and close to death. He has rejected his father and brother and put his trust in materialism and shallowness and been left to die far from home.

> A few days later the younger son gathered all he had and travelled to a distant country, and there he squandered his property in dissolute living. When he had spent everything, a severe famine took place throughout that country, and he began to be in need. So he went and hired himself out to one of the citizens of that country, who sent him to his fields to feed the pigs. He would gladly have filled himself with the pods that the pigs were eating; and no one gave him anything. (Luke 15:13–16)

At this point in the story we find ourselves.

Wasting Our Inheritance

It all began, innocently around 10,000 years ago, with the discovery that grain, if carefully processed, can produce both bread and beer. Bread gives humans a mild high and allows us to wean children younger and thus reproduce more efficiently. Beer gives us a comforting low and creates dependency. Grain is an opportunist; it can lie dormant for ages and grows when more sturdy plants have been destroyed by flood, fire, or human action. It was to human action above all that the fate of grain was most successfully hitched. Humans and grains became dependent on one another but at huge cost.

Unlike meat, berries, and edible leaves, this wonder-plant of civilization took goodness out of the soil without giving anything back. The more the land was worked at for grain, the weaker the soil became and the more land humans needed. Borders became frontiers of expansion as the first of our inheritance was laid to waste to support grain.

Since there is only so much good earth to conquer it is possible that we humans would have become extinct by now, but as luck would have it we made another amazing discovery. Deep in the earth were fossil fuels on which we could base our chemical fertilizers. We utilized huge underground water sources, which we could drill into, to re-irrigate the crumbling overworked earth.

This Green Revolution of the mid-twentieth century, as it was called, saved lives and allowed for even greater human reproduction. But this has only ever been a temporary solution. This revolution in agricultural technique was the second and most devastating stage of our alienation and wasteful misuse of our common treasury after our domestication of, and by, grain.

God has given the good earth as a common treasury for all but we have squandered it in material and political advancements that lead only to destruction. We know that we cannot go back in time and un-discover fossil fuels or agricultural farming or the green revolution.

What is done is done and the climate is in chaos as we try and throw off our habit of domination. We cannot go back but neither can we stay as we are. Carrying on as usual is like sleepwalking into a tsunami. The wonderful thing about Jesus' story is the son does find a way back. The son returns to his father despite the risk of rejection or punishment.

> But when he came to himself he said, 'How many of my father's hired hands have bread enough and to spare, but here I am dying of hunger! I will get up and go to my father, and I will say to him, "Father, I have sinned against heaven and before you; I am no longer worthy to be called your son; treat me like one of your hired hands."'
>
> So he set off and went to his father. But while he was still far off, his father saw him and was filled with compassion; he ran and put his arms around him and kissed him. Then the son said to him, 'Father, I have sinned against heaven and before you; I am no longer worthy to be called your son.' But the father said to his slaves, 'Quickly, bring out a robe – the best one – and put it on him; put a ring on his finger and sandals on his feet. And get the fatted calf and kill it, and let us eat and celebrate; for this son of mine was dead and is alive again; he was lost and is found!' And they began to celebrate. (Luke 15:17–24)

With the prospect of a miserable future he returned. But, before he can get close enough for indignant servants to kill him right there on the spot, his father rushes out to meet him and throw protective and welcoming arms around him. It is the returning that saves both father and son. And it is a journey home that we need to make as a human race in relation to the earth: our despoiled common treasury.

Coming to Our Senses

'Peak oil' is a term used to describe the moment when our natural inheritance begins to run out: when the amount of gas and oil we depend on is greater than the amount we can ever discover again.

We may have already passed that peak, or it may be just ahead of us; the reality is we cannot know. Peak oil is inevitable as we use more each day of a finite resource. The party is over but will we, like the son in the story, 'come to our senses' and return home? Will we make that journey back to a life more simple and resilient?

As our climate drastically changes and food and shelter become increasingly precarious, we are discovering that 'sustainability' is just another word for self-delusion. Since environmental shocks are inevitable, what we need is to find ways to be as *resilient* as we can to whatever future we may face.

Resilience and resistance go hand in glove. The most powerful systems in the world control our fuel and food. Just four companies, nicknamed the ABCD Group, manage nearly all the grain traded globally. Ninety-five percent of our food relies on fossil fuels one way or another. Resilience is our ability to absorb shocks as local communities. There are at least two shocks waiting for us: first, we have probably already passed peak oil and the price of food and fuel will only go up now; second, our climate is changing and the land will need to cope with increasingly extreme weather conditions.

People often try to find technological fixes that can allow us to sustain economic growth or materialistic lifestyles without depleting the planet's resources. Sustainability, it turns out, isn't sustainable. We will face a world with higher temperatures, and higher heating and eating bills until eventually, when we've finished fighting over whatever is left of the stuff they call 'black gold', we discover whether humans will survive: are we resilient?

Homecoming and the Welcoming Banquet

By creating local resilience we both enrich and empower the local economy and community and wean ourselves off the global markets that cast us aside at the slightest whim. Groups all over the world have begun to experiment with this kind of resistance and many of these groups call themselves 'Transition Initiatives'.[11]

A Transition Initiative, often located in a discrete geographical area like a town, estate, or other neighborhood, is an attempt to find local solutions to the global problem of oil dependence. These groups assert that powering down is both desirable and necessary and that we have the wherewithal to do it if we work co-operatively and look for a broad local consensus; shared wisdom.

The first Transition Initiative began in the town of Totnes, in the south-west of England. When I moved to Gloucester I discovered an emerging Transition Initiative focused around the city and there are emerging Transition Initiatives all over the country and around the world. What these groups are discovering is an ability to move from linear systems, where we find ways to manage the disposal of waste, to flow systems, which find ways to eliminate the very concept of waste. Rather than squander resources, Transition Initiatives try to let them be a borrowed gift, returning to replenish the earth and for others to inherit after us.

For those of us who have been taught in recent centuries that we are to dominate and steward over nature, this has been a tough call. We are invited to reconsider our position in relation to creation: distinct but no longer separate from the rest. We are returning home, having come to our senses, because we are realizing this blue-green planet is the home we left behind and the inheritance we have squandered. And in turning around and heading back into the protective and welcoming arms of creation we are discovering the earth's generous abundance – the feast that is a life well lived in community with all creation.

A Commonwealth for All

There have been other times and places where our alienation

from land and one another have been challenged. The 1650s heralded Britain's 'Commonwealth', as Oliver Cromwell's supporters did the theologically unthinkable and removed the head of God's representative on earth, King Charles I. The national experiment didn't last long but its legacy in local religious uprisings lives on in constantly renewed experiment. The dissenting radicals of the time included the Society of Friends, or Quakers; the Levellers; the Fifth Monarchists; the Diggers; and the Ranters.

Among these radical Christians were the 'true levellers' or Diggers led by Gerrard Winstanley. A prolific writer and Christian communist, his proposition that the land was a 'common treasure for all' led him to demand of Cromwell that he complete the revolution by throwing down the landlords and priests who exploited and fenced off common land.

Winstanley gathered about him a group of people committed to a simple experiment in common ownership and partnership. They dug the commons together and shared the fruit of their labors, each according to need. Sadly, this revolution was short-lived; the community was quickly and violently driven from the land.

But the legacy of the Diggers lives on: their music has been popularized by Leon Rosselson, Billy Bragg, and Chumbawumba, and in a very humble way their vision and their story has been recently revisited. Fewer than a dozen people, living in the rural and highly militarized county of Gloucestershire, England, meet in the form of a 'Diggers' Agape'.

The liturgy of the Diggers' Agape is based around some of Winstanley's writings, and the food and entertainment is brought by the guests; the only stipulation is that what we bring with us must be something that has 'never been bought or sold': a serious challenge in bleak wintry England where our dependence is almost entirely on supermarkets.

In our first attempt we gathered with some uncertainty; many of us brought things we felt were not entirely free. Some were more obviously free of the trappings of capital: surplus vegetables from a co-operative bio-dynamic farm nearby, a road-kill pheasant, some foraged greens, homespun foraged wool.

The group has developed in awareness of how our lives depend on a flagging fossil-fuel-hungry system. Little wonder we have turned to planning for action. In April 1649 Winstanley and his friends took spade to earth and began to change the world. Those who meet for the Diggers' Agape are inspired to do the same.

To gather and share of God's good earth, to dig the land, to hear some four-hundred-year-old wisdom read and prayed through into our own context, is a gentle invitation to a broad audience of Christians into a more honest politic and more concrete spirituality than Sunday mornings usually allow.

There are many directions a group like this might turn in the future: guerrilla gardening, seed bombing, orchard planting, Land Share, community agriculture, and others not yet thought up. What makes this a revolution is that the exchange of goods and labor are woven into the exchange of ideas.

A Journey Home

Paradise lost is paradise regained. We may not want to return to the 'innocence' of our pre-civilized world, although in the long term we may have little choice. Just as we have domesticated nature so nature has domesticated us. From the partnership's beginning, grain has exploited human desire and taken more of the earth from the perennial soil-nurturing plants that actively sustain the earth. Just as we have colonized and exploited creation so it has exploited us in return. Humanity cannot take full responsibility for the mess we are in since nature has always been our pliant partner in crime. Humans did not wake up one morning and decide, 'Hey, let's screw up the environment'; we, as products of our environment, responded to other environmental factors like fault lines that produce mineral-rich earth, animals that respond well to domestication, and annual plants that serve our evolving needs. We may be the only sentient players in the game but the chaos we have created has been a slowly developing change in human relations to the world around us. This matters because the temptation to hand-wringing and guilt-tripping is strong in many of us and may prevent us from seeing our worth as partners of creation that can turn around and go back home to a reconciliation with the world.

Like well-kept zoo animals we wouldn't survive very long in the wilds despite our sophistication and knowledge. What we need then is re-wilding or rather to become spiritually and practically feral communities. Uncivilized behaviors are a sign of hope because they remind us that there is more to human nature than our carefully constructed reality can contain.

Humanity has gone as far as possible in a linear understanding of the universe and has reached the end of the road. We cannot endlessly consume resources, produce waste and look for more resources. The political structures we have put in place to protect and serve us stand in the way of our journey home to a more respectful relationship with creation. Since the discovery of fossil fuels we have killed one another and our planet with increasing devastation and efficiency. Before all is lost we must regain our feral spirituality – let our spirits and societies name and challenge the myths of civilization – and the memory of freedom in order to begin a new journey: a journey home.

We turn now to look at how the systems act as messengers, shaping and dominating our experience of the world. It is not enough to create the change but it is necessary to see who the change-makers are and how and why they operate. In the following chapter we will look at the 'Domination System' as Jesus and his contemporaries experienced it. In doing so we will discover that his world was not so different from our own. Now, just as then, national and local elites manage the way the cultural symbols and systems that we take for granted persuade us to accept the way things are and even see those in power as being powerful on our behalf. We will explore the ways that ownership, the flow of capital, which we rely on for expertise, and the way information is censored all add up to produce a national culture that keeps us from trusting our own experience, relying instead on the powerful interpreters of the signs of our times.

Building Compassionate Communities

Suggestions for building a compassionate community of resistance where we are:

For Small Groups

Organize a 'Diggers' Agape' in your area. Write up the experience and share it with others. Send it to me too!

Further Reading

Rob Hopkins, *The Transition Handbook: From Oil Dependency to Local Resilience*, Green Books, 2008.

Mary C. Grey, *Sacred Longings: Ecofeminist Theology and Globalisation*, SCM, 2003.

Wilf Wilde, *Crossing the River of Fire: Mark's Gospel and Global Capitalism*, Epworth, 2006.

For more information, resources, and a chance to feed back your experiments and ideas, visit: www.compassionistas.net

9

The Domination System

Those who submit to those powers also are part of the violence under whose velvet terror we live and destroy others.
Dorothee Soelle

Herod's temple and its surrounding labyrinth were built to inspire awe and send a message of fear and fawning. The architecture and activity around the temple dominated religious and political meaning-making at the time of Jesus. The temple was the primary channel through which all debates must symbolically pass. For Jesus' contemporaries the place of the temple in their culture and geographical world must have been total in its normalcy.

The temple was the trusted home of God, God's footstool on earth, and people died to protect its holiness; most importantly the temple was a symbol of national pride. It was a sign of the people's defiance of Rome and their cultural independence. Rome allowed the customs of the temple to continue, mostly, with minimal interference, and any attempt to profane it was challenged courageously. It was the people's temple and their fortress against aggressive imperial forces.

You might wonder then why Jesus seemed so ambivalent, occasionally hostile, towards the temple. Jesus both worshipped at the temple and protested there. He called it God's house but also a den of thieves. He prayed there but claimed to be greater than the temple and prophesied its destruction. If Jesus were looking to start a popular revolution this would seem an odd way to go about it.

Yet Jesus saw something in the temple that his companions had not yet understood. It might project itself as the ultimate opposition to empire, but it was nothing more than the empire's agent. Its presence was dependent entirely on Roman largesse and peasant blood, sweat, and tears. Nationalism is the first recourse of a people threatened by globalization. Unfortunately the message and mechanisms of nationalism are easily co-opted by transnational super-structures.

Like the mainstream media today, claiming to be our trustworthy impartial truth-teller, defending us against the conspiracies of the powerful, the temple was beholden to four mechanisms that managed the message it sent out. The mechanisms were: ownership; income; expertise and censorship.

Ownership

The patron of the temple was Herod the Great who, although an overtly religious man, was known more for his cruelty, ambition and – above all – his dependence on the Romans who kept him in power. He was only able to massively renovate the temple on the backs of the poor and did so in order to ingratiate himself to the masses. Its physical presence spoke more of Herod's vanity than God's greatness. Jesus understood that the temple's brand-message was compromised by the source of its patronage.

Our mainstream media has its patrons too. Here are some of the biggest owners of western liberal media companies: General Electric (NBC, The History Channel), Westinghouse (CBS), Time Warner (CNN, 150 magazines), Disney (ABC News), and of course News Corporation (*The Sun*, *The Times*).

General Electric makes most of its money from war and nuclear power. Westinghouse also makes huge profits from nuclear power. Disney's backers have an appalling human rights record, and profits rely on our dependence on fossil fuels. Time Warner was a major backer of George W. Bush's presidential campaign. At the time of writing, of the top ten shareholders in News Corporation eight are investment banks, one is a Saudi prince, and the 'mafia' godfather, Rupert Murdoch, takes the lion share of shares.

Jesus sought an alternative media to the temple. These alternatives are agents of change rather than channels of the mystique of the powerful. Jesus claimed that he – a human being – was greater than the temple. Like the Pharisees he encouraged people to think for themselves, to take religion into their own home, to be empowered beyond the expensive cultic faith of Jerusalem.

For compassionate activists, finding ways to encourage and generate local independent media is an important way to divest the systems of some of their power locally. By looking beyond the headlines to the power-players behind the media we can more clearly understand what the overall message is and whether it is helpful or not.

Although through publicity stunts and shock tactics we can sometimes shoehorn a glint of reality into the mass of media propaganda, we will not effect real change by occasionally getting an alternative message into the mainstream. Local newspapers, book groups, conversations with neighbors, coffee mornings, union meetings, mooching in our own community are the ways in which an alternative propaganda can be made real for real people. You and I will never have the power of the media, thank God, but we will have the opportunity to listen to our neighbors and be alongside the isolated and forgotten.

Income

People say Las Vegas wasn't built on winners; well, nor was the Jerusalem temple. It was built on the tithing of the people and the costs they bore for practicing religion. The original purpose of tithing was to create a reserve of wealth so that in times of crisis the poorest would not be left vulnerable. It has been a model borrowed by the modern idea of the welfare state.

However, like the welfare state, the Jerusalem temple had been misused, leaving many vulnerable people to fall through the welfare gaps. The centralizing of welfare is a mechanism that leads to the distancing of the cared-for from the care-agent. The system that was intended to distribute wealth becomes self-serving, self-preserving, and ultimately self-defeating.

The temple also made huge profits from the religious observances of the people. At times when a culture feels threatened by an outside global force, local or national culture gains new importance. This is one reason for the Europe-wide rise in nationalism and the rise of what people call Islamism in other countries. People feel under siege.

The renewed temple worship in Jesus' time was a great money-spinner for Herod as well as for the priestly caste and their administrators. Temple money changing and the cost of buying unblemished animals for sacrifice led to a financial monopoly on religious devotion. The temple authorities had no reason to challenge the status quo. The protective authorization from the Roman-controlled kingdom of Herod suited them very well.

It has long been the case that the money spent buying a newspaper doesn't cover the cost of its production. That cost is met by advertising. In order to make money, news agencies must attract advertising. In order to attract advertising they must be careful not to annoy the corporations. Because it is the advertisers and not the readers who make news journalism a going concern, it is they who matter most. The readers become important only in their ability to attract advertisers. This means the more affluent the readership, the better the advertising revenue. It stands to reason, in such a culture, that nobody will want to write for or about people without spare cash or credit.

Our media, politics, and education system all reflect the language of the powerful. One of the reasons literacy is so low amongst low-income households is that there is very little incentive to read. They are barely visible in the media and patronized in fiction. So the media does not act as their voice in opposition to power. Little wonder most press agencies are happy to use asylum seekers, single mothers, and Muslims as scapegoats for an unjust system. These are people who the advertisers aren't interested in keeping on side.

Publishing ideas is expensive and the greater the cost is, the more likely it is to be corrupted by the values of the powerful. Local worship, storytelling, live music events, Zines are all ways to re-invigorate the local media. The parish magazine used to serve this purpose in much of Britain. As the Church declined in importance most churches have not partnered with others to re-widen their understanding of the word 'parish'.

Most regional newspapers are owned by international media companies and are held back by the same constraints, so genuinely local people writing for and about themselves can begin to create a new language and build a new symbolic world for those who are normally ignored.

Expertise

The temple authorities were in charge of how reality was described; they faithfully guarded and nurtured the traditions, stories, and rites of the people. They were the experts on whom the grand narrative of society relied for its reinforcement. They were the interpreters of the signs of the times and mediators of the politics of religion. There is always a politics of religion of course but the closer that political view is to that of the ruling consensus, the less obvious it is.

Jesus repeatedly challenged the ruling consensus by engaging in confrontational conversations with their representatives. Using parables and riddles he invited everyone to join the conversation; to find their own solutions. In other words, he democratized expertise. No wonder he was such a threat. If Jesus had set himself up as another expert he could be easily dismissed, but if he chose instead to unleash the expertise found in authentic community then one cannot so easily dismiss ninety-nine percent of the population.

One group of people working to change all that are the staff and supporters of 'Ekklesia'. Ekklesia is a think-tank with an ever-deepening influence and a stubborn refusal to take large donations. The paid staff all earn far less than the taxable minimum, and much of the work is done by unpaid volunteers who believe in what Ekklesia are trying to achieve and their values:

> Ekklesia seeks to reinvigorate a different understanding of the church as an alternative-generating 'contrast society' within the wider civic order: one that is hospitable, politically aware, intellectually curious, spiritually refreshing, theologically rooted, voluntarily associational, actively nonviolent, and radical in its social commitment.[12]

One of the most popular demands of the Occupy Wall Street movement as it emerged in the autumn of 2011 was 'Take the money out of politics'. The movement was completely ignored by the mainstream media for weeks after it first began and when they finally reported on it they misled the public with phrases like 'These people don't know what they want!'

Taking the money out of politics is one thing; taking the money out of ideas is another thing entirely. Perhaps this is why the Occupy London Stock Exchange developed a 'Bank of Ideas' in a disused investment banking office. Once ideas are set free, much that was thought impossible becomes achievable.

Censorship

Our final mechanism for managing the message of the institutional structures is censorship. Censorship can be either open punishment or implicit harassment. Among the more obvious forms of censorship of ideas were imprisonment, torture, and crucifixion. Crucifixion was a favorite among the Roman rulers because it offered a gruesome public punishment for dissent.

More subtle means of censorship were enforced through the religious purity codes that set some people apart as ritually unclean. These people were kept outside the community. This meant they were unable to speak of how their distinctiveness was made a disadvantage by the society they lived in. They included those with imperfect skin, those who hemorrhaged, and those who did the sorts of jobs that others wouldn't want to do.

Another form of censorship came obliquely through the dismissive attitude that the ruling elite had to ideological groups that challenged the status quo. Blasphemers and Zealots were more generally feared or derided. These terms of general abuse were a quick way to shut down a line of thinking that appeared subversive. Jesus' detractors accused Jesus of blasphemy and of being in league with demons. They often tried to trap him with their questions into taking an ideological position that they could deal with: Should we pay taxes to Caesar? (Are you a collaborator?) Should we heal on the holy day? (Are you a heretic)? Should we stone this adulterer? (Are you a nationalist?) But Jesus turned each challenge around on the accusers in order to show how far they had gone from their ethical heritage.

Labels like these serve to dehumanize opposition. Instead of seeing those whose views we hate as human beings, just like us, we often look at them as labels. Labeling others is often a form of violence against their personhood and legitimate needs.

After the overthrow of the Russian Tsar in 1917 the terms 'red', 'communist', and 'anarchist' became popular pejorative for the first time in the USA. They were used to dismiss the views of anyone or any news outlet that stepped out of line. To this day in the USA the term 'socialist' is used as a term of abuse. Those who fear others are almost always the origin of a social label. The terms 'Christian', 'anarchist', 'Hindu' and 'black' all started out as dismissive, abusive, or pejorative terms long before the groups so labeled began to accept them as self-descriptors.

To move beyond such labels is a constant challenge. Sometimes it is enough to find a suitably vague or valueless term like 'activist' or 'community organizer' but any label can be misappropriated and always is.

Over the past few decades we have seen movements rise and vanish. 'Reclaim the Streets', 'Critical Mass', 'Antiglobalization', 'Green' and 'Occupy' are all terms that have value only so long as they denote action rather than ideology. It is this focus on action rather than abstraction, brief rather than belief, that has allowed these movements to avoid the trap of becoming organizations and institutions that can be co-opted, censured, and dismissed.

Agents of Change

In Jesus' world of Roman occupation the agents of national pride were covert messengers of the occupying force. It remains true that the institutions and organizations that we trust to challenge the powerful rely often on the same systemic worldview as those they seek to challenge. This renders the opposition incapable of affecting seismic change.

Real change never has its origins at the center of power but always at the edges. That's why unions are unable to break the power of the owners of the means of production. This is why national news agencies can rarely move the debate beyond narrow parameters. Those who wish to be agents of change must begin by changing themselves. Or as Gandhi put it, 'Be the change you want to see in the world.'

We cannot be the change without the help and support of the communities we live in. In fact authentic human 'being' only really happens when community is fully realized. So to be the change we want to see in the world we must find ways to be the communities we want to see the world made up of.

The mechanisms by which the powers shape, and limit, debate are ownership, income, expertise and censorship. Our response to the owner-agents of this world must be to enable local leadership where distant rule has failed to deliver. Our response to the backers of the ruling consensus must be to refuse to make sacrifices of the innocent by glorifying or sanitizing war or paying for the propaganda of the powerful by reining in our dependence on the big media giants for information.

Our resistance to the authority of the experts can be found in our commitment to the wisdom by finding our own consensus through deepening community where we live and work, and we challenge censorship by finding new ways to speak out and new ways to challenge the dominant jingoism of our day. By doing all this we become agents of change and begin to take back some of the power from the ruling consensus. We begin to tell our stories for ourselves.

All this resistance to the domination system begins and ends with listening to and supporting locally. If you have read the gospels through, you may have noticed that Jesus listens to and stands alongside a whole spectrum of people: whether tax collector, beggar, army officer, or imperial ruler, Jesus treats each individual and starts with where that person is, not where he wishes they were. If, like Jesus, we can work with a whole continuum of people, always with an eye to moving people from enemies of change to agents of compassion, then we can begin to work as part of wider movements that will also change us. In the next chapter we will break down Jesus' interactions into four groups along a single continuum. We will then explore the different needs that each group has and how Jesus responds to those needs.

Building Compassionate Communities
Suggestions for building a compassionate community of resistance where we are:

For Small Groups
Choose your most trusted media source and see who advertises

in it and find out who owns it. What does this information tell you about how the choice of content is made?

Further Reading

Noam Chomsky and Edward S. Herman, *Manufacturing Consent: The Political Economy of the Mass Media*, Vintage, 1995.

Naomi Klein, *Fences and Windows: Dispatches from the Front Lines of the Globalization Debate*, Flamingo, 2002.

For more information, resources, and a chance to feed back your experiments and ideas, visit: www.compassionistas.net

The Compassion Continuum

*Unity, participation, and solidarity always include a rejection of
everything that separates us, all that divides and breaks up life.*
Dorothee Soelle

In the gospels we have a Jesus who engaged with a whole
continuum of people in different ways. In any attempt at social
activism there is a range of positions of both power and
perspective to attend to. There are those who understand the
goals and make natural comrades. There are those who have the
most to lose and set themselves up as enemies. Always Jesus met
people where they were and invited them to go further;
sometimes they did the same for him, challenging his ideas and
preconceptions.

To keep things simple we will divide these into four groups,
a spectrum of enemies and allies that mirror the variety we
experience ourselves when we engage with any community. At
one end of the spectrum are the natural allies, the disciples; then
there are the crowds of ordinary people with sympathies for
Jesus' ideas but not quite bought in; then there are the professional classes who have much more invested in the present
system than poorer folk; finally the client rulers: the real enemies
of social change.

Reality is always more complicated and fluid than any
continuum can handle. Ordering things as above helps us understand that different people have different needs and start from
different places. In order to effect real change it is necessary both
to engage people wherever they are in the spectrum and help
them move to larger and more irresistible alliances for change.
With honesty we always need to consider our own position in

relation to change since we all, by degrees, have much invested in the status quo.

Jesus and the Disciples

We begin with Jesus' natural allies. The disciples have made a serious commitment in relation to Jesus personally and to his vision as they see it worked out. Jesus' work with a core group of activists focused around creating an intentional community sharing some form of common purse as well as common ideals. These were people who, to a lesser or greater extent, understood what the compassion of God was about and were able to do the things that Jesus did both with Jesus and in small groups.

The way the gospel writers present things, it often looks, at first glance, as though Jesus was doing everything and the disciples were just looking on. This wasn't the case. Take the example of the story of Jesus cleansing the temple courts. The temple courts were a huge area: crowded and full of people selling animals for sacrificing at jumped-up prices and temple moneychangers taking advantage of poor pilgrims.

> Then they came to Jerusalem. And he entered the temple and began to drive out those who were selling and those who were buying in the temple, and he overturned the tables of the money-changers and the seats of those who sold doves; and he would not allow anyone to carry anything through the temple. He was teaching and saying, 'Is it not written, "My house shall be called a house of prayer for all the nations"? But you have made it a den of robbers.'
> (Mark 11:15–17)

The gospel writers tell us that Jesus did four things: he turned over the tables of the moneylenders, he drove out the animals, he blockaded the exits, and he taught the crowd. All this was done in full view of the authorities and Roman guards in their watchtowers.

Although the gospel writers tell us that Jesus did all these things, there is no way he could have acted alone. This was a pre-planned group-led disruption of business to give a message to the people. When we read 'Jesus' in the gospels it is often short hand for 'Jesus and the disciples' with Jesus being the story-teller's focal point. Jesus engaged with his disciples by teaching them through direct action as above. He also taught them through parables, easily remembered sayings, and through a common prayer life.

The Crowds

For Jesus and the disciples, direct action and prayer go hand in glove; so do teaching and caring. There is a crossover between what is said just with the disciples and what is said to our second group: the crowds.

One of the most radical forms of intervention Jesus used was to heal people on the Sabbath: the holy day of rest. In order for a political elite to maintain social control over the crowds, there must be a class of people who are outcasts. These are the people that the crowds fear to associate with and dread as signs of their own future if they don't work hard, pay their taxes, and keep their noses clean. By touching and healing the outcasts Jesus reintroduces them to the crowd, removing fear of them with love.

For Jesus the words 'sin' and 'debt' were interchangeable. By forgiving sins Jesus was reminding the crowd and the horrified wealthy lenders that they have forgotten God's command to keep the Jubilee and fifty-year Sabbath. The Sabbath and Jubilee years were part of the ancient priestly code (Leviticus 25 – 27): every seven years all the land is rested and all debts are forgiven. Every seven-times-seven years, all land is returned to its original keeper. It was like a social reset button, making adjustments for the inevitable widening of gap between rich and poor. By forgiving people on the weekly Sabbath rest day, Jesus reminds everyone that we can only rest when the world is at rest – when peace and justice are achieved. The day of rest follows six days of re-creation, not six days of oppression.

As well as economic intervention, Jesus taught the disciples and crowd principles and methods of nonviolent resistance and gave them parables in order to provoke them into analyzing their own situations for themselves and coming up with their own solutions. In Matthew's gospel chapters 5 to 7 we hear Jesus giving a step-by-step guide to creating a community of resistance in his list of blessings and in his treatment of morals as an ethic of human worth: we hear him encouraging the crowds to internalize the spirit of the law instead of fearing the letter of the law. With the parables we hear Jesus take ordinary rural life to tell stories with unexpected twists and turns that leave the listeners asking one another, 'So what *is* the compassion of God like?'

Teachers, Merchants, Officers, Temple Priests

Turning to the professional classes, this category of people is divided into two: those who were sympathetic to Jesus' vision and values, and those who were suspicious of or antagonistic to the cause. With the antagonistic group, public debate and confrontation were the two methods initiated by both Jesus and his enemies. But for the sympathetic professionals, private conversations were necessary.

Among those who were the sympathetic elite, one would count a Roman centurion with a sick servant, at least two Pharisees called Nicodemus and Joseph, and a synagogue leader whose daughter had died. But one striking example would be the nameless Canaanite woman who came to Jesus for healing but met with the sharp end of his tongue.

The woman was from a wealthy district of the empire, famous for its trading ports serving the known world. Very different from Jesus' homeland of Galilee, a fertile rural area that grew grain but whose peasant farmers could barely afford to eat. Much of the grain was exported to the rich coastal towns at prices that Jesus and his friends could barely afford.

Here was a huge contrast then between farmers who grew the bread but could not afford to eat it and those who were so wealthy they used bread as napkins to wipe their sticky faces and then throw to the dogs. And whatever the dogs did not finish, the poor people could sneak away with.

So when this wealthy woman came to Jesus we should not be too surprised at the rudeness of his response: 'Why should I give to dogs what is meant for the people of God?' The challenge to her position of privilege was ruthless. He has reversed the story so that the rich foreign rulers were the dogs and the indigenous poor were the ones with the bread that was theirs to give or keep.

The woman has a choice: she could revert to type and point out that Jesus and his friends should know better than to speak to her that way. Or she could take his challenge seriously and explore the word-picture he had given her. She chose the latter: 'But even the dogs may eat the crumbs from under the table.' In that simple phrase the woman showed that she knew the situation of the poor and she knew that it was unjust. Her faith had made her well, and the humanizing of poor people had begun her on the road to healing from her alienation and from her dehumanization.

The gospel writers tell us of a couple who, when caught in adultery, were separated and the woman dragged into the street and paraded before Jesus in mockery. Notice that the adulterous man has not been dragged out. The scribes and Pharisees challenged Jesus on his religious credentials and tried to trick him into either breaking the cultural law – stoning the adulterous to death – or defying the imperial law – only Rome was legally allowed to execute anyone. 'The Law tells us she should be stoned' they said. 'What do you think, Jesus?' Jesus responded with a challenge: 'Let the one who is without sin throw the first stone.' From the eldest to the youngest (I wonder if her lover was among them) they put down their stones and went away. Jesus turns to the un-named woman and affirms that no one is left to accuse her and sends her away to 'sin no more'. Jesus has again exposed the sacrificial system where a marginalized innocent victim is created. This was not a moral judgment against her but rather a challenge for her to live by.

Jesus would often give a direct challenge to the ruling elite. In the Apostle John's version of Jesus' life and purpose there are two events that inaugurate Jesus' ministry: the miracle at the wedding and the temple protest. The inclusion and pairing of these events make sense since the former challenges domestic exclusion and the latter challenges state exclusion.

Jesus attended a wedding with his mother and friends (John 2). It is a typical wedding following all the rules of behavior of that culture. For example, before entering the wedding you must wash ritually in a particular way, otherwise you are not able to take part. Anyone who didn't know how to do it properly probably would not be invited anyway so it is rarely something people make a fuss about. Jesus had not been intending to make such an overt challenge just yet: 'My time has not yet come' he says to his mother.

The wedding hits a crisis as the wine begins to run out and Jesus is given an opportunity he feels compelled to take. Focusing in on the ritual water jugs gives the story an interesting twist. The Pharisees knew that for the national religion to mean something in the daily lives of ordinary people it had to escape the cultural monopoly of the temple system and enter their homes. Ritual washing of hands and crockery in particular ways was part of this domestication of religion. However, for Jesus the message of the ritual was very different. When criticized for not following these rituals he points out that it is not the outside ritual – known only to those who can afford such things – that make a person holy or unholy, but rather it is what comes out of the heart. By making this claim Jesus takes the seat of holiness out of the realm of human judgment and into the far more important realm of God's judgment. Ritual would cease to separate insiders from outsiders. So these symbols of religious and social exclusion he turns into the finest wine – a wonderful symbol of joy and welcome. And how could his hosts complain since their greater need was to keep the wine coming for their guests.

So many things are exposed in this story: the abundance of God, the hypocrisy of the host and his willingness to compromise his religion, the rituals of exclusion themselves. But it is in relation to the client rulers that we look at Jesus' temple protest below. In John's gospel this story is put at the beginning of Jesus' public ministry and alongside the cleansing of the temple, showing it to be a pattern for his relationship with the professional classes.

Client Rulers

We come to a final social grouping: the client rulers. These are represented by kings' stewards, tax collectors, temple priests, client kings of national descent but imperial loyalty, and of course Pontius Pilate the Roman procurator of Jerusalem. These people are the social network represented by palace and temple as the physical centers of a domination system.

So it is to the temple that Jesus must eventually go, in order to expose and confront the powers at their spiritual heart. There are many accounts of Jesus challenging the powers but this event – which is the climax of Jesus' ministry, or its inauguration depending on which version you read – stands out in its explicit and aggressive challenge to power.

I am going to use St Mark's version again here because it is the oldest, likely to have been written about thirty years after the death of Jesus, and because it has slightly more detail than John. It is worth reading the whole exciting event:

Then they came to Jerusalem. And he entered the temple and began to drive out those who were selling and those who were buying in the temple, and he overturned the tables of the money-changers and the seats of those who sold doves; and he would not allow anyone to carry anything through the temple. He was teaching and saying, 'Is it not written, "My house shall be called a house of prayer for all nations"? But you have made it a den of robbers.' And when the chief priests and the scribes heard it, they kept looking for a way to kill him; for they were afraid of him, because the whole crowd was spellbound by his teaching. And when evening came, Jesus and his disciples went out of the city.
(Mark 11:16–19)

Although the passage reads 'he' and 'Jesus', a lot of it must have been a pre-organized team effort. Direct action of this kind takes planning with a trusted 'affinity group' who work out roles and timings in order to create the maximum impact in the quickest time: before the authorities have time to react and suppress the protest.

Mark frames this event in prayer-warfare. Before they go to the temple Jesus and his disciples curse the fig tree, a symbol of national wellbeing, for not producing fruit. On returning from the direct action they discover that the tree has indeed withered.

The way the protest event is sandwiched between this cursing and denouncing of the spirit of the temple, that is the fig tree, shows how integral prayer and action are to one another in compassionate activism. But what it also shows is that Jesus and his disciples are willing to expose their political convictions so publicly as to threaten the existence of their movement in order to bring about a more universal change of perception and put pressure on the elite.

Systems under Pressure

In any challenge to the powers a key task is identifying 'who's who'. There are those with the least power who need to come alive to the way the powers rule their lives; those with some power and the beginnings of awareness but no tools or organization with which to resist. Finally there are the powerful, some of whom will have uneasiness about the roles they find themselves in and may be open to change. Identify these people – as much as possible by name – and find together the best way to work with them in order to put pressure on them to shift to the place of ally or to stand down from their position of facilitating injustices.

There is always fluidity and complexity in this but creating a simple matrix from which to begin to act is helpful to any program for change. This was Jesus' approach and it is why he used parables that described real-life people and their power relationships in order to get everyone to work this out for him or herself.

Much of the book so far has been an exploration of the way we understand unjust systems and respond with spiritual insight and compassion. We turn now toward the important role played by direct confrontation with the monsters and messengers. Because confrontation requires self-discipline and a community who trust one another it is helpful to have agreed methods and principles. We begin with some methods of what I am going to call 'shalom resistance'. Returning to the word *shalom* – often translated as 'peace' – we are reminded that any confrontation with the systems needs to be in the context of seeking God's peace. God's peace is different from the peace of the world which is based instead on the pacification of dissent. For God's peace to be made actual it must be complete and inclusive of all systems, all people, and all creation. Shalom resistance can never be about subduing the unjust systems but transforming the situation so that – to cite Jesus' interpretation of the prophet Isaiah – 'the stars will be falling from heaven, and the powers in the heavens will be shaken' (Mark 13:25). We will be exploring five tried and tested methods of shalom resistance: 'Prophecy', the speaking out of God's justice; 'Lament', the public mourning and repenting of injustice; 'Meek Refusal', those acts of disobedience that clog up the mechanisms of unjust systems; 'Direct Action', interventions that either symbolically or actually prevent injustice; 'Subversion', turning upside down the worldviews of the powerful.

Building Compassionate Communities
Suggestions for building a compassionate community of resistance where we are:

For Small Groups
With others, try using the continuum in relation to a local struggle for justice. Name people and groups who are known to you and place them along the continuum. Consider how Jesus might respond to each and how that informs your action.

Further Reading
Paolo Freire, *Pedagogy of the Oppressed*, Continuum, 2001.
Anne Hope and Sally Timmel, *Training for Transformation: A Handbook for Community Workers*, Vol. 1/3, Mambo, 1984.
Saul Alinsky, *Rules for Radicals*, Vintage, 1989.
Dave Andrews, *Compassionate Community Work: An Introductory Course for Christians*, Piquant, 2006.
Stephen Pattison, *Pastoral Care and Liberation Theology*, SPCK, 1997.
Alistair McIntoch, *Soil and Soul: People Versus Corporate Power*, Aurum, 2004.

For more information, resources, and a chance to feed back your experiments and ideas, visit: www.compassionistas.net

11

Methods of Compassionate Resistance

Oneness with God, beginning in action, can discover the mystical unity that undergirds resistance.
Dorothee Soelle

The five methods of compassionate resistance offer a broad canopy within which to work. I can't call this definitive and wouldn't want to. I invite you to critically work through these and think of your own or rework them in ways that makes sense for you and your community. The methods of compassionate resistance described in this chapter are:

1 Prophecy
2 Lament
3 Meek Refusal
4 Direct Action
5 Subversion

The five methods of resistance draw on ways Christians have often chosen to resist injustice from a particular point of view: a shalom point of view.

Shalom is the wholeness that comes from living justly with our neighbors; it is the healing that takes place when we are in proper relation to the land, one another, and God. Shalom is the peace of God that goes beyond words into corporate experiences of wholeness and justice. It is this shalom that we prophesy, lament the loss of, and refuse to give up, speak and directly bring about. It is this shalom that subverts the peace that the unjust systems offer – the transient, pacifying peace that we experience much of the time while having that nagging feeling within us that life was never meant to be this way – that there is something better.

Prophecy

Prophecy is a useful place to begin because it is within the biblical tradition. But the meaning of the word has been somewhat confused. With the privatization of religion has come the privatization of the message of the prophet. To prophesy is to discern the times we live in in relation to the justice of God. It is to get to the root of the matter in a creative, spirit-led proclamation first to ourselves as groups, and then to the systems.

When the system tells us that salvation lies in being healthy, wealthy and wise *individuals* – thus proving we are blessed by God – so the prophets that are heard are those that promise us this kind of salvation. They are the politicians who tell us that recovery is on its way, the marketing companies that sell us a dream life at the price of a new phone, the telly evangelists who tell us we will be healthy and wealthy if only we trust God and buy their products.

Authentic prophecy is rarely possible outside of a prophetic community experiencing being in the forgotten places of empire. It is only in community that we begin to move beyond our selves into the realm of the spirit and into what Dave Andrews calls 'intersubjectivity' in which God's truth is found in the creative space between our many points of view and tells us both how things are, the direction we're going, and the changes needed.

Prophecy is about the broader strokes of God's vision and hope for creation. It lies in the ability of marginal groups to identify the sickness of our society and, through prayer and discernment, begin to map out God's alternative.

Imagining a new world and beginning to build it in the shell of the old world is the final outworking of prophetic community. Catholic priest and prophet Philip Berrigan wrote, 'The poor tell us who we are and the prophets tell us who we should be. So we hide the poor and kill the prophets.' Prophecy can be a risky business as the biblical prophets bear witness.

Prophecy is an essential tool in waking up others and us to present realities and new possibilities. The faithful and regular presence of survivors of the bombing of Hiroshima and Nagasaki outside the gates of a nuclear warheads factory in Berkshire alerts the prophetic community to the pressing need to challenge our government's illegal and immoral commitment to building more and bigger nuclear weapons. I have been an occasional visitor to the Atomic Weapons Establishment (AWE) over the last few years but for some it has been a place of compassionate resistance for more than six decades.

Trident nuclear missiles are built and maintained at a site in Hertfordshire, the AWE. At any one time a Trident submarine, armed with nuclear missiles, patrols international waters with the capability of deploying nuclear warheads up to eight times more powerful than those used against Japan in 1945. Nuclear warheads offer no practical defense in war and deliberately target civilians.

International agreements bind the UK government to work for disarmament and not to increase the number of weapons. However, nuclear weapons act as a guarantee of great influence in the UN Security Council and are used by the UK as an implicit threat, rather than as a defense, against other nations. According to the Geneva Convention on conduct in warfare, it is illegal to deliberately target civilians. Nuclear weapons are designed to target vast civilian populations so they are both illegal and by any standard immoral. This means that any action to intervene to prevent the building, maintenance, or use of nuclear weapons is not only legal but also something we are invited to do. This is why, despite many arrests of protesters over the years, rarely do interventions go to trial.

My first visit to AWE was on Good Friday of 2007. My wife, our daughter and I met with three others to form an affinity group, committed to some form of prophetic action in relation to the site. Two of the group, Les and Liz, brought with them both experience and particular gifts in artistic vision and play. We met, huddled around a coffee table in someone's front room. Liz, a fantastic artist, brought out some maps of the site, with all the inner detail removed, and spread them in front of us. She then produced a box of crayons and pens, inviting us to re-imagine the site as what it could be instead of what it currently is. Like the spies who entered the Promised Land we were to go to AWE and bring back a good report. Like a reverse of Don Quixote we were to look at monsters and imagine them as windmills!

We enthusiastically set to work. The most inspiring and unusual coloring-in came from the two-year-old in the team. We drew a deer sanctuary, some permaculture design, a brewery, and even a mosque and peace center. We replaced all the factories of death with signs of life and a renewed economy for the whole local community. We had fun.

After further discussion and prayer, we assigned roles within the group. One was experienced in presswork and was to stay at the house (as was the toddler) to pray and get the story out. Two were to be in support roles, driving to the site and to the police station if necessary, and liaising with the home support. The final two – Les, a marine veteran and I – were to climb the fence at AWE and begin to peg out the new world we had imagined together.

All went well until we tried to climb the fence. I hadn't thought too much about this moment apart from choosing to wear old painting trousers that I didn't mind getting torn. Les was considerably fitter and had no trouble with the fence. I went first and managed to get halfway over before getting my crotch stuck on the barbed wire. In what was one of my less elegant maneuvers, Les managed to get my other leg over the wire so I could make it, coughing and spluttering, to the other side. Then he bounded over to join me.

As soon as we were both over the fence we got to work: spying out the land for development opportunities. We had brought with us stakes labeled with the things for the renewed site. We began to place these wherever we felt best around and about.

We had only been there a few minutes when a group of Japanese people with cameras passed us on the other side. We waved and they waved back. It turned out they were Hiroshima survivors who were there for a blockade of the site taking place the following day. These were people who knew what it meant to be on the sharp end of the state's posturing and violence.

When we had been over the fence about forty-five minutes, amazed at how much surveying we had managed, the MOD police arrived. At first it was one man with a dog and a gun; which for me is plenty. But in minutes we were surrounded by seven police officers. We followed instructions to the word: dropping our rucksacks and putting up our hands. But we also took the opportunity to involve the police in our work. One officer suggested five-a-side pitches and quite a few liked the idea of an open-air jacuzzi with a bar (which was where they arrested us).

The police were very polite and gentle throughout, even asking if my handcuffs were too tight and shutting off the fan in the van because they thought it was making me cough. But they did insist on locking us up; which isn't so polite.

If the police interview you it usually means they don't think they have enough evidence to make charges stick. You have three choices: tell them everything; tell them nothing (usually a good idea); or play with them. I chose to play; it's my default option. If the incident went to court the transcript would be read out so it would also be a chance to put forward the prophetic message behind the action. You join us part way through.

'Did you see any signs on the fence telling you not to go in?'

'No, I didn't. I saw a horse though. Oh, and a sign that said

"Bikini".' (True, by the way.)

'But the fence must have indicated that people weren't allowed in.'

'But people are allowed in; there are seven gates into the site.'

'Those are for authorized people working on site.'

'We were working. We were doing a survey...'

'But you've already told us you know there are nuclear weapons in there so you must realize the fences are there to keep people safe.'

'Oh? No, no, no. Nuclear weapons are usually attached to rockets. They can go right over fences.'

(Sigh.)

'Interview terminated at...'

It was the evening of Easter Day; I was released to go off to the pub and wait for a lift back. I had spent much of my few hours in the cell praying and singing hymns. I was deeply aware that, in other countries, we would not have been treated so well for such cheek. A friend and refugee from the Democratic Republic of Congo noted that if he'd done that in the DRC he'd have been shot before he got near the fence. I was also aware that what had happened was only possible because of an affinity group and prayerful support: vital in any context.

Eventually, the Crown Prosecution Service (CPS) decided there was not enough evidence to convict and after six months on bail, going back and forth to Newbury police station, the charges were dropped. The CPS are a constant source of frustration for arresting officers but their job is not to decide the guilt of the offender but the likelihood of conviction on the evidence. Meanwhile we built up a good relationship with our arresting officer, Mike, and had a prophetic story to fire up others who might also imagine a world with something better than nuclear weapons.

A small affinity group, with imagination, can have the impact of hundreds of marchers. They can also be an opportunity for adventure and what community theologian Ann Morisy calls 'a story-rich life'. This is, essentially, the prophetic life.

Lament

Public crisis often invites the enactment of public drama or lament. Lamentation is beyond sadness, despair or grief. It is the public and deeply felt response to injustice or tragedy. The feared closure of a public library has already provided one example of effective lamentation, not because it was a library but because it was yet another example of government prejudice against an under-represented community. The public lament of the universal tragedy of the re-occupation of Iraq by western states and corporations provides another example.

When a large group of students and local church representatives, in the center of Birmingham, lamented the re-occupation of Iraq, no anti-war statements were made. The names of the dead were read out – both Iraqi civilians and Allied forces – and these were interspersed with a slow drumbeat and readings from the prophet Jeremiah's 'Lamentations'.

John Hull, along with other staff and students at Queen's Foundation in Birmingham, has been working with students and trainee ministers over the last decade committed to transforming unjust structures. Lamentation has become an important part of the work they do. For John Hull and others, lamentation has the advantage of bringing together more people than an ideological protest might.

The public mourning for the conflict's dead became an annual part of the Foundation's public Christian witness and has included a procession and placing ash on the heads of participants and onlookers as a sign of repentance and mourning. In a culture where public grief is beginning to emerge as socially accepted and recognized, this is a powerful way to reveal and engage with deeply felt loss.

Individual and communal laments play an important part in the biblical witness. They aid the oppressed in their attempts to make sense of the social chaos that comes from being squeezed or crushed by those in charge. Lamentation can express both resignation and tenacity; both accusation and restoration. They are a coming together of three great traditions: wisdom, prophecy, and ritual.

Many people in the west find the book of Psalms (songs and poems for gathered worship) a difficult read because of the violence they express, but this raw exploring of our internal violence is most uncomfortable to those of us who realize that it is the voice of the most marginalized crying out against the rest of us and against God for letting all this happen: 'Why?!' and 'How long?!' wails the psalmist, asking the taboo questions of our spiritual, political, and philosophical worldviews.

Lamentation psalms show a basic structure that may prove useful for contemporary activists: a cry for help; a deep mourning; a turning to God; a specific plea; a vow of praise. It should not surprise us that lamenting oppression is not peculiar to the psalmist. In India the Dalit communities know of lamentation too. The Dalit communities, who are sometimes called 'untouchable' or 'outcaste' and are often forced into degrading labor, have begun to speak out against their political and social conditions. Some Dalit people have begun to make use of the arts to express their discontent. Dalit Christian activist Manohar Prasad cites this example of a Dalit poet expressing horror at the daily tragic deaths among Dalit people:

O Beloved we have witnessed your death
we call for revenge
Dalit legions will gather like fire flames
O my beloved
before our blood drains from our body
We Dalits will not spare those who trampled us
we turn into red flowers for revolution.
Laxmi N. Barwa[13]

The Dalits, meaning the 'crushed of the earth', are those in India who are considered unclean by birth and polluting by contact. There are around 400 million Dalits in India alone and many are in bonded labor and involved in degrading or dangerous work: tanning leather, street sweeping, removing human waste manually, and so on. They are almost always landless and segregated, especially in rural areas.

I met recently with Manohar, a South Indian priest and activist, in his office in central Bengaluru (Bangalore). Manohar is a Dalit and a determined champion of the rights of the Dalits whose spiritual and political solidarity with the oppressed are integral to each other. He told me of a community of Dalits whose job it was 'to carry human waste in containers on their heads' in order to regularly clear out sewer systems. If this was not degrading enough, local developers decided that the scrubby land these people lived on was of value and the Dalits must be moved on. To ensure this they cut off their utilities and encouraged local people to abuse them. 'If there's something worse than being a shit-shoveler it is being a shit-shoveler with no access to water for washing!'

Instead of buckling under such pressure, and despite generations of learning to quietly acquiesce, this community chose to publicly lament. In the heat of the day a small group of men arrived in the dusty square outside the town hall. They arrived with wide-brimmed shallow containers of human waste balanced precariously on their heads, exposing to the public witness the nature of their work, work that is formally illegal but still socially enforced. If this was not lamentation enough, they then smeared the excrement over their heads, clothes and bodies; allowing the stinking waste to dry and crack in the sun. How does that compare with signing a petition for getting a point across?

None could doubt the reality of the oppression, or the sincerity of their lamentation. Like the widow who nagged at the unjust judge (Luke 18:1–8), like Jesus' call to remove your tunic with your cloak and stand naked in view of your oppressor (Matthew 5:40), these Dalit people knew how to bring a God-view of oppression into the realm of the powers. This reminds me of the ancient tradition we find in the Bible of ripping clothes, refusing food, and covering oneself with dirt (Jonah 3:6). It is a dramatic outward sign of a corporate lamentation.

Not all acts of lamentation are so extreme. They often offer people who are hesitant about protest a way of expressing themselves without a confrontation point of view being expressed. At Queen's Foundation some students had already been to AWE and to another weapons site in Scotland but never as a large group. We made it our aim to go to AWE as a whole coachload of people, most of whom had never been involved in anything remotely like this before.

Because lamentation had resonated with so many people already, we decided to take this approach again, and after much discussion we hit upon two very visual acts of lamentation: smearing of ash on our heads and fastening of red and white poppies onto the perimeter fence of the site. This would be accompanied by reading names of the dead, a sermon from Bishop Steven Cottrell, then Bishop of Reading, where the site was located, and an address from someone who had visited Hiroshima.

The event was carefully planned and we did our research on the legality of our actions. This turned out to be vital as the police were deliberately misleading as to what we were legally allowed to do and we had to hold our ground, politely but firmly. In the end they did not interfere with our legal right to express ourselves and even gave the coach a police escort from one of the perimeter gates to the next because the driver wasn't sure where to go! The event was extremely moving for all involved and for many it was an opportunity to reassess their views on our continued development of illegal and immoral nuclear weapons.

Lamentation can be transforming for those who choose to lament and those who attend as observers. It is also a spiritual activity and its intercessory role should be valued in its own right. When we lament we accuse God, we accuse ourselves, and those whose behavior creates fear or injustice. We ask the questions 'Why?' and 'How long, O God?' and our prayers tune us in to the will of God, hastening justice. Often lamentation leads to direct actions and story-rich lives that transform the lives of others and create a new national ethos that can lead to real political change. Public lamentation, like public mourning, offers a rich, diverse, and creative way to tap into the spirituality of anyone and everyone to bring about real justice.

Meek Refusal

If you've ever looked after children – your own or those of someone else – you have probably witnessed meek refusal at its most effective. Children are experts in nonviolent resistance. They have to be, since anyone who gets between them and another biscuit is going to be bigger and stronger. Here are some of the favorites that I've collected from friends:

- 'Cuddling and refusing to let go'
- 'I love you, Mummy – even when you're cross!'
- 'The general art of faffing plus wanting to do something entirely different to what's on offer!'
- 'Wee-ing himself in awkward places... lying on the floor howling – sorry, lamenting...'
- 'Blowing her dad a kiss [my three-year-old niece] from the naughty step'
- 'Distracting me with random requests for a story'
- 'Nonviolent resistance to going to bed: needing extra kisses, stating random fears that need resolving, wanting more stories/songs/prayers...'
- 'My younger daughter has always ignored anyone saying

anything she didn't want to hear... but open a packet of chocolate buttons under a duvet at the other end of the house, and she is there in seconds!'

- 'My daughter frequently uses the "sit-in" technique or the "make yourself go really floppy and slippery" one.'
- 'Silence; refusing to eat'
- 'He picked up chocolate that he knew he shouldn't have, marched straight to the naughty stair, sat down on it and announced, "Don't worry, Mum, I'm eating it on the naughty stair."'

And just so that you know that the children aren't the only ones with the gift, here's a quote from a member of the Christian Peacemaker Teams (CPT):

I used nonviolent resistance against a toddler... does that count? I was visiting some friends during a break in my CPT training. I went upstairs to read the littlest one a bedtime story and mummy came up too. I was sitting on the bed with baby... and the book. Mummy said, 'Can I sit down too?' Baby answers 'NO!' So, I sat down on the floor with mummy until baby could agree that there was space on the bed for everyone. I suppose it was really solidarity with parents. Don't mess with CPT, kids.

Meek refusal, sometimes called non-compliance, has been an important tool for industrial struggles and political resistance throughout history. So it is no surprise that it turns up in the biblical tradition too.

Take the Hebrew midwives in the exodus saga, for example (Exodus 1). The Hebrew people have been domesticated as a slave caste within a powerful empire: forced into backbreaking labor and political impotence. The ruler of the empire becomes concerned that a new generation of Hebrews may get political and rise up against him. So he orders the Hebrew midwives to kill all newborn baby boys on arrival. The midwives seem to have two options: follow the orders or protest them. But they choose a third option, passive disobedience. To be meek is not the same as to be passive.

To be meek is to show restraint in one's actions. Meekness allows for a measured and therefore more productive response to oppression. This is why Jesus said that the meek shall 'inherit the earth' (Matthew 5). Jesus knew that those who can restrain themselves from merely reacting to someone else's agenda will find a way to have their hunger for justice more completely satisfied.

So what do the midwives do? Well, at first they just don't comply: they let the babies live. But the emperor is not going to sit back and watch his orders ignored. He is both a man and a God and they are only women and of the slave caste. He demands an explanation.

The midwives said to [the emperor], 'Because the Hebrew women are not like the [local] women; for they are vigorous and give birth before the midwife comes to them.' So God dealt well with the midwives; and the people multiplied and became very strong. And because the midwives feared God, he gave them families.
(Exodus 1:19–21)

He gets an explanation: the Hebrew women are too strong and give birth before the midwife can arrive. Now tell me, *Mr Emperor*: what do you know about gynecology then? Care to contradict? I didn't think so. No doubt this explanation would not have washed with the emperor but it stood nonetheless as the barefaced but sidestepping resistance of violence and oppression. The Hebrew people were not yet in a position to escape completely from the grip of empire so they had to try every trick in the book to work the system just to survive for now.

In Norway, under direct Nazi administration, when in 1941 the government tried to force professional bodies to join up, they met with meek refusal on all fronts. The athletics groups disbanded, unions refused and forty-three professional bodies signed an open and joint declaration against compulsory membership of the Nazi Party. This resistance was met by violent recriminations, prison sentences, and repression that triggered 'mass resignations from the organizations and, far from weakening them, gave them new vitality'.[14] Schools and churches joined in with their own resistance; bishops and teachers setting the example of public refusal were sacked but continued to publicly defy the Nazis, leading to a massive climb-down from the fascist regime.

Throughout Europe, but especially in those regions where Jewish people were fully integrated into wider society, civilian resistance saved more lives than military combat could ever hope to lay claim to.

Despite the overwhelming success of meek refusal compared to Allied military force, cultural rituals in Britain perpetuate the state-sponsored myth of redemptive violence. This is because our governments know that if people got wise to the power of meek refusal, their rulers, elected and otherwise, would not be able to oppress, exploit, or ignore them anymore.

Direct Action

In February 2003 over a million people took to the streets of London to show our disapproval of the re-occupation of Iraq. We believed that our government's reasons for attacking the country were a pretext for occupation of the territory and exploitation of its mineral resources. Marching didn't work, as we now know. The invasion took place, no weapons of mass destruction were found, and Tony Blair started inventing after-the-event arguments for why the war was morally justifiable. Despite being widely held to be a war criminal, Tony Blair and his associates continue to profit from that decision. It was the magnificent failure of that march through London that led me to realize that traditional protest is not creative or costly enough to lead to change.

Sometimes it is necessary to take action that may at first glance appear violent, but that is only because so many cultures have come to value property over people. Were I to smash a door down, it might be considered an act of violence. Were that the door to a room full of people and that room was on fire, it would be a different matter. The Ploughshares movement is an international and de-centralized movement of people committed to taking direct action to save lives by getting in the way of state-sponsored violence, even if this puts them at odds with governments. The Ploughshares movement take their inspiration from the words of the prophet Isaiah.

In days to come
the mountain of the LORD's house
shall be established as the highest of the mountains,
and shall be raised above the hills;
all the nations shall stream to it.
Many peoples shall come and say,
'Come, let us go up to the mountain of the LORD,
to the house of the God of Jacob;
that he may teach us his ways
and that we may walk in his paths.'
For out of Zion shall go forth instruction,
and the word of the LORD from Jerusalem.
He shall judge between the nations,
and shall arbitrate for many peoples;
they shall beat their swords into ploughshares,
and their spears into pruning-hooks;
nation shall not lift up sword against nation,

neither shall they learn war any more.

(Isaiah 2:2–4)

Participants in a Ploughshares action take an almost literal approach to this prophecy by acting it out, not on swords, but on machines of modern warfare. During the re-occupation of Iraq by British, US and other state forces, Ireland took a position of formal political neutrality or so the Irish government claimed. In fact Shannon Airport became an important stopping-off point for US military aircraft on their way to Iraq.

Late one chilly February night, an affinity group of five people broke into a hangar at Shannon and disabled a US Navy transporter. Having used hammers and mattocks to disable the plane, the five laid down their tools to pray and await arrest. Their joint statement of faith began with the words, 'We come to Shannon Airport to carry out an act of life-affirming disarmament in a place of preparations for slaughter.' They were soon arrested and removed from the scene.

Their actions cost $2.5 million in damage but more importantly it meant the plane could not complete its mission of death. Untold numbers of civilian lives were saved directly by this action but equally important were the political implications that unfolded.

When I first met Ciaron O'Reilly, who was one of the five, it was about a year after the event. The verdict on his actions that night had not yet been finalized and he was looking at the possibility of ten years in jail if found guilty. O'Reilly, a Catholic Worker community member and a part of the Ploughshares movement, said then, 'If only five percent of those who marched against the Iraq War directly intervened we'd be in a very different situation today.' O'Reilly argues out that if those five percent end up in prison and the other ninety-five percent supported those prisoners and their households then we could have stopped that war.

We could end all war with that kind of commitment and we are that many in number; it's just that we rarely organize ourselves well enough to resist. For British communities a lot of that is about a cultural leaning towards gently mocking cynicism in relation to any strongly held conviction. We marginalize activists as eccentric. Really eccentric is our refusal to acknowledge responsibility for the way things are: that is truly eccentric. But every now and then we come together and draw a line. That is when the compassion of God is near.

What was most important about this story was that a jury of their peers acquitted each and every one of them. Their defense was that they had a moral and legal duty to intervene directly in a war that was illegal and immoral, and the people of Ireland sent a strong message to their government with the jury's verdict of 'not guilty'. Direct action does not always have such a clear outcome and many people have faced fines and prison sentences because of their conviction that they must do something.

Subversion

In the section on lamentation we have begun already to look at how use of text can be used to re-imagine situations. By text I mean both word and image; image is a major way that propaganda works its way into our value-systems and it was just as important in Jesus' context. The subversion of the propaganda of the powers is a creative component in the struggle to transform unjust structures.

Christians often use the word 'evangelize' to describe telling people the good news about Jesus. But where did this word come from and what might it mean? The word has a pre-Christian usage and relates to the propaganda of the Roman Empire. It has a similar meaning to 'decree' or 'royal announcement' or even 'advertisement'. Knowing this pre-Christian use of a word helps us to figure out why it was adopted by the early churches. As we will see, the early churches were adept at taking the propaganda of the empire and using it in new and creative ways to usurp or subvert the official messages of the powers. We have already seen something of this with Jesus' cursing of the 'fig tree', but there's a whole mountain of other ways in which the saints achieved this turning upside down of the word.

St Paul's writings demonstrate that subversion of language was a key tool in the early church's propaganda of the text. As well as being a founding missionary for the Church, Paul was known for two things: first, his conversion from being a reforming Jew to being a Jewish mystic follower of Jesus; and second, his pastoral letters. He was so famous for his letters that even after he died people wondered what he might write about their situations and penned letters in his name. I am going to focus on the letters about which there is a consensus that they were written by Paul.

These letters are 1 Thessalonians, 1 and 2 Corinthians, Galatians, Philemon, Philippians, and finally Romans. These seven letters cover roughly a decade of activist letter writing and are broadly self-consistent. These are the letters of radical Paul, the Paul who was arrested, put on trial, and almost certainly killed for his values and activities along with St Peter in Rome. This is also the Paul who witnessed the persecution of Jews across the Roman Empire and saw their return to Rome to find that non-Jewish followers of Jesus held sway in the small Jesus-following communities there and were not keen to share power with their Jewish brothers and sisters. This Paul witnessed and detested the violence and debauchery of Roman rulers and their vile propaganda.

Despite his long letters, Paul chose his words carefully. Take, for example, this quote from his letter to the Thessalonians: 'They say "There is peace and security," then sudden destruction will come upon them.' The phrase 'peace and security' was a favorite propaganda catchphrase of the Roman Empire who taught that only by their sword would peace come to any barbarous peoples.

For the Romans, peace meant pacification. It would be like commenting in Britain in 1997, 'They say, "Education! Education! Education!" but they will learn only the wrath of God!' Your listeners would be in no doubt that you were referring to the New Labour propaganda that led many schools into impossible building debts and privatized many of the poorest schools by handing them over to businesses and interest groups.

When Rome went out to war and pacified another people group, it felt the need to parade that victory to its own citizens back in Rome. The spoils of war – people, animals, and material goods – would be marched through the city. The crowds would gather, cheer, and throw rotten food and stones at the new slaves, and everyone would be reminded of how great and blessed the Peace of Rome was. This was an awesome and terrible sight and very different from Jesus' provocative return to Jerusalem on a donkey, waved in with palm branches and cloaks. Paul then, perhaps familiar with the story of Jesus' 'Palm Sunday', takes this language and applies it directly to Jesus: in contrast and defiance to the Roman Peace he places the Peace of Jesus, one that involves forgiveness and restoration rather than pacification and theft.

One of Paul's favorite words is the Greek word *parousia*, usually meaning 'return of a victorious military ruler', and it marries with another word, *apantesis*, which often means 'meeting with a returning dignitary'. The following quotes from the first letter to the Corinthians and the Thessalonians illustrate this well (italics mine): 'Christ the first fruits, then at his *return* those who belong to Christ' (1 Corinthians 15:23) and 'Then we ... will be caught up in the clouds together with them *to meet* the Lord in the air' (1 Thessalonians 4:17).

The opening of Paul's letter to the Romans offers multiple examples of how the author takes the language of empire and subverts it.

[T]he gospel concerning his Son, who was descended from David according to the flesh and was declared to be son of God with power according to the spirit of holiness by resurrection from the dead, Jesus Christ our Lord ...
(Romans 1:3–4)

There are three key words here showing Paul's usurping of Roman domination and monopoly on all public space: 'gospel', 'Son of God', and 'Lord'. There are also political overtones to the claims 'descended from David', which challenges Roman authority, and 'Christ' which is a resoundingly political term.

Some people play down the political language in the New Testament, claiming that Jesus' followers misunderstood Jesus to be a political leader when he was more a spiritual leader. There is no evidence for this, but many of us have been so completely brought up with the idea that religion and politics must be kept separate that it's hard to imagine religious conviction as anything other than an individual or private concern. Jesus' explicit intention, worked out in Paul's letters, was for a spiritual and political revolution; he knew nothing of the modern distinction between the two.

Each of the phrases Paul uses has a political meaning that predates its Christian meaning. A 'gospel' is a Roman edict, for example, one that announces the birth of an heir to Caesar. Rulers were often thought of as divine in some way, and this theology of kings reached a high point with the Roman emperors who were often called either gods or sons of God. Finally the word 'Lord', which in English is also a political term but because its use is archaic it has been fenced off as a spiritualized description of Jesus that is also individualized. So Jesus becomes 'Lord of my life' instead of an alternative to politics as usual.

To some extent we can recognize the language of the Roman Empire in the rhetoric of our own political systems: 'peace and security' have always been the buzzwords of dictators. In his final few weeks in power in Egypt Hosni Mubarak claimed that he would love to resign as leader but, if he did, the Muslim extremists would cause chaos for everyone so he needed to remain dictator for the sake of peace and security. Governments, at their basest level, tend to operate like the old-style Chicago protection rackets; they create fear and then offer protection at the price of loyalty and taxes.

But the powerful are always creating new phrases to go with new ways of presenting the same old ideas. They turn up in ministerial speeches as though they've always been there; soon they are in books and papers as though we have always known about them: Big Society; War on Terror; Homeland Security; Commonwealth; Economic Wellbeing; Multiculturalism. But it isn't just government: 'Because you're worth it'; 'I'm lovin' it'; 'The real thing'; 'Just do it'. International corporations do the same. The list goes on. No doubt you could think up many more.

We have the same opportunity that St Paul and the apostles did to take this language and subvert or co-opt it to either reveal its true meaning or give it a deeper, more transforming meaning that speaks of God's view of reality. Below is an excerpt from a liturgy that has been used at an event at AWE.

> Leader: Our war on terror
> Voice: is perfect love (1 John 4:18)
> **All: With this, we resist!**
> Leader: Our homeland security
> Voice: is the commonwealth of Christ (1 Corinthians 10:16)
> **All: With this, we resist!**
> Leader: Our citizenship
> Voice: is in community (Acts 2:44)
> **All: With this, we resist!**
> Leader: Our peace
> Voice: is in the reconciliation of the cross (Romans 5:10)

All: **With this, we resist!**

This way, we can reclaim language from the powerful and visual images from the dehumanizing exploitation of desire by the big marketing companies. We can turn mourning into dancing.

One of the most popular examples of this is the work by the group Adbusters. People from Adbusters take television adverts and billboards and make subtle changes to them in order to reveal something of the truth behind the superficial and deceptive message of the company selling you its goods. Adbusters tend to target fast-food giants, multinational drinks companies, and car companies. One of the brands that Adbusters have taken on is Camel cigarettes, replacing their child-friendly cartoon character 'Joe Cool', a cigarette-smoking camel in a baseball cap, with their own 'Chemo-Joe', the same cartoonish character in a hospital bed on a ventilator. The cartoon image has been heavily invested in financially by the company, and Adbusters took all that emotionally targeted branding and turned it on its head. Take a look at some of their work on the website: www.adbusters.org. The Christian traditions are full of powerful phrases and images that can match those of the powers if only we use them to full mischievous advantage.

Building Compassionate Communities
Suggestions for building a compassionate community of resistance where we are:

For Small Groups
Guerrilla gardening! Find a forgotten piece of land in your community (start small) and plant it up with something beautiful, something edible, and something symbolic.

Further Reading

Harry Browne, *Hammered by the Irish: How the Pitstop Ploughshares Disabled a US War-plane – with Ireland's Blessing*, CounterPunch and AK, 2008.

David Augsburger, *Caring Enough to Confront*, Regal, 2009.

Online

Trident Ploughshares Movement:
http://www.tridentplough shares.org/
The Speak Network: http://www.speak.org.uk/

12

Principles of Compassionate Resistance

Prison can be where the human being is found in an inhuman world.
Dorothee Soelle

The six principles of compassionate resistance draw on ways in which M. K. Gandhi's and Jesus' principles overlap. Leo Tolstoy's understanding of the Sermon on the Mount inspired Gandhi to develop his own practice of nonviolent 'Truth-Force' in order to help the struggle equality in South Africa and for self-rule in Colonial India. The principles of compassionate resistance are:

1   Create the Future
2   Love the Other
3   Integrate the Self
4   Initiate the Engagement
5   Consent to Loss
6   Die to Self

Principles bind a community of resistance together and increase trust. If the principles from which a group work are shared ones then, even if there are disagreements as to what methods are appropriate, they can be worked back to shared principles so that we can understand one another's reasoning. Principles allow us to take action in ways that are unlikely to compromise the group intentions when events move quickly around us. In other words, whether you agree that these six principles are useful, having an understanding of what principles your group works by makes it much more likely that you will work effectively together and be able to reflect meaningfully on any action and prepare for the methods you choose.

Create the Future

First, *Create the Future*, as an equal to the enemy, with dignity. Gandhi caught the imagination of all kinds of people by using direct action that challenged the status quo with a vision of a more just future. In 1930 Gandhi led a march to the Indian coast, challenging colonial tax-theft. As he held high a lump of salty mud he said, 'With this I am shaking the foundations of the British Empire.'

Gandhi and his companions were protesting against what they saw as an unjust tax. At that time it was illegal for Indians to make their own salt yet they were taxed heavily on the salt they bought from the empire. The result was greater hardship for the poorest to the benefit of the wealthy and powerful.

Looking back at this historically significant event, we would do well to remember that the British Empire was not centered at Dandi beach. Until that day it is likely that most British administrators would have struggled to find it on a map.

Perhaps Gandhi was advised by his friends on how to tackle this injustice: 'Go to Delhi and dump a sack of rice over Lord Irwin's head!' 'Support our military insurgence!' 'Send a petition to London.' But Gandhi did none of these things nor in any other way lobbied the colonial powers. He understood that in this case the power for change lay in the hands of the people through making their own salt, thus rendering the salt law impotent. In word and action, Gandhi encouraged rural Indians to become self-sufficient through weaving and stitching their own clothes. Gandhi did this at a time when Britain was trying to impose a trade monopoly on a global textile market.

One day Jesus went to a well during the heat of the day, a time when only social pariahs were likely to be there, and engaged in conversation with a woman his community were traditionally at odds with. When she challenged him on their religious and social divides he painted a picture of a very different world where institutions would no longer be gatekeepers of social and spiritual worth: 'the hour is coming when you will worship the Father neither on this mountain nor in Jerusalem' (John 4:21).

Sophie and I were visiting friends in North Wales when we heard the news of the huge nonviolent protest by monks in Burma. Burma is a longstanding totalitarian regime, shaped by colonial powers and then left to local despots. Nonviolent resistance to the system is ongoing and courageous. These efforts are not helped by the fact that the energy monster Total have a huge investment in the country, despite its appalling human rights. Many people in the UK responded by blockading Total petrol stations in order to highlight the link between our support of Total and Total's support of a dictatorship. We felt we wanted to respond too but in a different way.

We decided we would get material in the five colors of Buddhist prayer flags (blue, white, gold, green, and red) and encourage passers-by to write prayers and messages of support on them. We would then hang them up in the streets and hold a candle-lit vigil. Each step of the process would involve us in engaging informally with members of the public on the issues and how they relate to us. We asked Birmingham Cathedral if we could use their railings but were refused for reasons of 'health and safety'. The police refused to allow it on public highways either. In the end we chose to do it anyway on a busy Birmingham shopping street.

Within five minutes of setting up, a local police sergeant turned up and told us we could carry on as long as we liked and to let him know if anyone bothered us. Around four hundred people helped the dozen or so volunteers to write, draw and hang the flags on street furniture. We had messages from people of all the major world faiths and others from people of good faith. There was color, hope, and diversity as well as defiance, challenge, and silent vigil. The event raised the profile of the cause of the Burmese freedom fighters through conversation, ritual, and – through good presswork – the prime spot on regional BBC News. It also built up trust for future activities, including from some who had declined to support the event.

But that wasn't the end of the story. A few days later a Burmese pastor was visiting the city and was able to take the flags back with him. The following year a group in Bradford joined the two ideas together. They made the flags with local Buddhist communities and then used them to create a more effective and visually impacting blockade of a Total petrol station. The situation in Burma shows great signs of change, including greater freedom of speech and organization, and the global campaign and awareness continues to apply pressure on Total and on governments.

Creative activism is addictive and contagious because creativity always generates further creative acts. Play, imagination, carnival, and the exotic are all ways to keep the energy going and bring a new vision of a just society to a world grown weary of marches, placards and angry exchanges of views. Have fun. Too much activism is polemic or drains the life out of those most involved. Finding new ways to surprise ourselves, and others, keeps the momentum up and gives us the stories to help us through more difficult times.

Love the Other

Second, continue to value and *Love the Other* while boldly declaiming oppressive acts. This is only possible if, as Gandhi counseled, the resister can both organize public opinion against the violence of the enemy and yet deal honestly with what good one finds in the character of the enemy. In other words the aim should always be to redeem the enemy, not damn them.

Jesus pointed out to his listeners that God allowed the rain to fall on the righteous and the wicked alike. He counseled indiscriminate compassion.

But I say to you, Love your enemies and pray for those who

persecute you, so that you may be children of your Father in heaven; for he makes his sun rise on the evil and on the good, and sends rain on the righteous and on the unrighteous. For if you love those who love you, what reward do you have? Do not even the tax-collectors do the same? And if you greet only your brothers and sisters, what more are you doing than others? Do not even the Gentiles do the same? Be perfect, therefore, as your heavenly Father is perfect.
(Matthew 5:44–48)

This challenge to others was equally so for Jesus who was willing to help a Roman centurion, a wealthy landlord, tax collectors, and self-righteous leaders. Jesus' wholesale compassion caused endless controversy because he refused to be pigeonholed, owing allegiance to God and to all God's creation without prejudice.

My experiences of British policing have varied from getting callous indifference or violence to warm-hearted patience and kindness. Like most people, I have tried to be consistent in my own attitude to police. We are all working in, and compromised by, the same system. This is true of politicians and police officers as much as it is true of judges, solicitors, and hippies.

Personally I have found this hardest when talking with Christians with extreme views or who fund violent and hate-filled organizations. Getting beyond the prejudices to hear and love the person behind them, and thereby getting beyond my own prejudices, is a constant challenge.

By choosing restraint, kindness, and grace we refuse to give violence of language or action the prime spot in desires. This is a revolutionary choice in itself. As well as being a revolutionary choice it can lead to surprising results. When a large group of us arrived at Aldermaston in a coach, the military police were understandably disconcerted. We had done our research though and knew both the law and its consequences. This meant that when the police lied to us about what was and wasn't legal we were able to politely but firmly explain what we were going to do and why it was not illegal. Not only did they choose not to arrest us but when we said we were going to protest at the next site and our coach driver didn't know the way, they offered a police escort and a nice spot for our pack lunch. Love wins.

Integrate the Self

Third, *Integrate the Self*. Gandhi urged resisters to be model prisoners if arrested for civil disobedience and to accept arrest, yet he also taught them to resist anyone who took property entrusted to them. He maintains this tension through a certainty that surrender takes more courage than fleeing or flailing. One of the first reforms that Gandhi undertook was of his own practice. In his early experiments with Truth-Force Gandhi chose to start cleaning his own toilet. For someone who had been told all his life that this task was materially and spiritually polluting, this was more challenging than it sounds.

Gandhi came to believe that calling people 'untouchable' because of their occupation was wrong. In order to live out that belief he experimented with doing some of the untouchable tasks. Gandhi never quite got over his upbringing but made a serious commitment to the journey. Whereas many of us assent to something before we do much about it, Gandhi's 'experiments with truth' committed him to practice what he hoped one day to preach.

Jesus reflects this confidence throughout his dealings with his aggressors, both Jewish and Roman, and it is summed up in his response to Pilate, 'You would have no power over me unless it had been given you from above...' (John 19:11a). In his final meal with friends, Jesus chose to wash their feet. This was a task normally taken on by a female slave. In a mix of cultures where patriarchy was so strong this was a role that male teachers would never take on. But Jesus had consistently taught servanthood and was determined to demonstrate bodily what he believed in heart, soul, and mind.

When I preach I am constantly challenged by the words of Dorothy Day, founder of the Catholic Worker movement: 'I have long since come to believe that people never mean half of what they say, and that it is best to disregard their talk and judge only their actions.' Catholic Workers strive to integrate the self through what is called 'Round Tables of Discussion for the Clarification of Thought'. These are group sessions where honest self-examination in a trusted group setting is encouraged. For all of us, a rhythm of contemplation or a regular and examining liturgical life encourages the integration of the moral and spiritual self. We cannot respond in the heat of the moment with integrity that we haven't plumbed for in the consistent quietening and examination of the heart and mind. Like Gandhi we can commit ourselves to experiments in truth.

Initiate the Engagement

Fourth, *Initiate the Engagement*; use surprise as a weapon. When arrested in South Africa, Gandhi asked for the maximum sentence, one that the judge could not bring himself to impose. By doing this Gandhi highlights the absurdity of the charge and the injustice of the law against the authentic judgment of the marginalized. Gandhi asks his supporters not only to avoid violence but to defend their enemies from the violence perpetrated by others: an act of self-sacrificing love for the enemy.

Jesus urged occupied citizens to carry the pack of an occupying soldier an extra mile, thus voluntarily extending their own suffering. Jesus' parable of the Good Samaritan shows the active love of the enemy as an exemplary ethic. The marginalized Samaritan not only helps the suffering enemy but also goes as far as possible to help him, taking every opportunity to love him and show him acts of mercy.

Ray Gaston is an interfaith enabler working in Birmingham. As a parish priest in Leeds he was committed to interfaith relationships that had pastoral and political implications. He was also committed to a spirituality of resistance. This meant that at the re-occupation of Iraq by Allied forces he felt compelled to disrupt civic peace in the way that real peace was disrupted for Muslim and Christian brothers and sisters abroad. He used his body to block a busy road in and out of the city.

After his arrest, Ray remembered Gandhi's example; he chose not to accept a caution and when presented to enter his plea in court he knelt in the dock:

> Rather than stand before you, I prefer to kneel, not to the authority of this court, but to the authority of God, who is the Creator of the universe and the lover of our souls … Let us pray for the people of Iraq, that they may know the love and mercy of God as bombs rain down on their land and homes … [15]

At the end of the prayer he and others sang the Kyrie (Lord, have mercy) and a poem was read out from the public gallery. There is no point at which options are not available to us. We have been nurtured to conform to expectations and to see our real choices narrowed by them. There is a liberty to taking captive each moment and finding in it both human dignity and personal volition.

Consent to Loss

Fifth, *Consent to Loss*. Be willing to suffer rather than retaliate and face penalties rather than uphold unjust laws. Both Gandhi and Jesus recognized that surrendering to the desire to match violence invites domination. So Gandhi advises, 'Put up with assaults from the opponent; never retaliate.'

Jesus offers the ultimate illustration of willingness to suffer, one which offers the cornerstone of the nonviolent paradigm in Luke 17:33. 'Here also the cross is the model: we are liberated, not by striking back at what enslaves us – for even striking reveals that we are still controlled by violence – but by a willingness to die rather than submit to its command.'[16]

The enemy, in reality, is the desire to control others through violence, but equally through the threat of violence. This means that a soldier who holds a gun is as culpable as one who fires it, since both perpetuate the myths that superior force equals moral rightness.

As I write this, a friend is in prison. He's in and out of prison so often I'm almost getting used to it. Fr Martin, a member of the London Catholic Worker movement, is prayerfully committed to living alongside asylum seekers and to bearing public witness to the systems that put them there. No one minds when a Catholic priest chooses voluntary poverty but they do mind when he brings our attention to the causes of poverty. Dorothy Day, the founder of the Catholic Workers, was fond of quoting another priest, Dom Helder Camara: 'When I feed the poor, they call me a saint. When I ask why the poor have no food, they call me a communist.' There is a great cost to service and an even greater cost to integrity.

Die to Self

Finally, *Die to Self*. Death to self, both as a way of living that embraces death in spiritual contemplation, and as a willingness to die, helps maintain a vision of the compassion of God. Die to fear of your enemy to take the sting out of his violence and to make him ashamed of his actions. This is evidenced both in non-compliance with unconscionable laws and refusing to react violently to those who impose them.

Gandhi, in one breath, urges Indians neither to salute the Union Jack, nor insult the colonial agents. Holding these values together allows the person resisting evil to maintain her humanity in the face of evil. In the context of General Dyer's massacre of protesters in Amritsar, he wrote: 'The might of the tyrant recoils upon himself when it meets with no response, seen as an arm violently waved in the air suffers dislocation.'[17]

Throughout his experiments in truth, Gandhi held one objective in mind, the 'conversion' of the enemy, through non-violence to repentance.

This is an attitude reflecting that of Jesus, who taught his disciples to use the shame of having their outer garment taken by richer debtors, to bring to their attention the horror of what they are doing to another human being. This unmasking can lead to a forced change of behavior on the part of the oppressor or even a conversion of the enemy into an ally. If the enemy is converted to God's solidarity with those on the margins, then they are set free from the violence without falling into violence themselves.

Building Compassionate Communities

Suggestions for building a compassionate community of resistance where we are:

For Small Groups

Jesus said, 'For which of you, intending to build a tower, does not first sit down and estimate the cost, to see whether he has enough to complete it?' (Luke 14:28). Inventory: What are you willing to risk or lose? What is there to gain? Compare your inventories, discuss, and do another inventory as a group.

Further Reading

Chris Howson, *A Just Church: 21st Century Liberation Theology in Action*, Continuum, 2011.

Crimethinc Workers' Collective, *Recipes for Disaster: An Anarchist Cookbook*, Crimethinc, 2005.

For more information, resources, and a chance to feed back your experiments and ideas, visit: www.compassionistas.net

Conclusion

Ordinary Compassion Begins at Home

Ordinary compassion begins at home and resistance begins in the heart. Compassionate resistance to the monsters, messengers, and oppressive systems begins locally and always returns to the local. Public, radical compassion is as joyful as it is costly. This mirrors the compassionate activism of Jesus who devoted most of his time to the everyday acts of compassion and generosity among the poor local neighborhoods where politics was as parochial as it was framed in a global empire. Although Jesus is best known for taking the struggle to the regional center of empire, he always returned to the shores of rural Galilee to teach, to the fields, plains, and hills of Caesarea, and the first priority of a resurrected Jesus was to return to Galilee and begin the struggle all over again in the community that was reborn in the execution of its leader.

Compassion begins locally because the greater our social cohesion, the better equipped we are to offer alternatives to the smothering and theoretical unity imposed by corporations and the state. Not one of us has the solution to any of the complicated challenges we face. It is only together, in the margin of translation between Thou and I, Jesus will draw us into the compassion of God.

By beginning locally we refuse to give in to the scapegoat mechanism when we refuse to lay hands on the scapegoats, instead celebrating the wisdom and insight that they bring from the edges of society to the rest of us. Resistance begins locally because, as Gandhi once said, we need to 'be the change that we want to see in the world'. We can only practice social revolution; we cannot pass it through parliament or lobby to be transformed by the renewing of our minds.

Compassion returns to the local because only through a refocusing of politics on the local and personal responsibility can we resist the ever distancing of power away from the person at home or in the street. By creating local alternatives to institutional solutions we move away from the sort of peace that works through domination and pacification, to a sort of peace that works through personal accountability and community-led programs of restoration and restitution. Compassion returns us to our neighbors because that is where the cycle of resistance begins again. Because there will always be those who take power away from us, we will always need to wrestle it back and rediscover the power of us.

Public compassionate resistance is joyful because it leads to solutions and visions that no single person can imagine without the public meeting of minds and wills. It is joyful because it needs to be. Through creativity, fun, pleasure, and re-invention of ourselves, we can maintain the great energy needed to carry on, despite the frustrations and great costs. As the activist and writer Emma Goldman puts it: 'If I can't dance, I don't want to be part of your revolution.'

Public resistance is costly because those who offer a wisdom which is foolish to this age put themselves at risk of slander and ridicule. At times senior officials in my diocese have dismissed my 'arrogance of youth'. I have been accused of anti-Semitism because I refuse to stand back when Christians exploit Israelis and Palestinians for their own twisted ends. I have been assaulted and jailed. And I consider myself to have got off lightly. Many thousands of people who practice the necessity of nonviolent resistance work at great personal cost in the UK as well as more oppressive regimes.

Just as Jesus' most revolutionary message is in the way he lived his life, so Gandhi discovered that the most revolutionary act is the one that is independent of the state. How do we challenge the systems? Creatively seeking first the compassion of

God. The monsters are not afraid of marches and placards; they are afraid we might outgrow them and turn our backs on them – and our faces to one another. Many people have said this before, better and more simply. In fact as Lao Tzu, founder of Daoism, beautifully and simply states:

If there is to be peace in the world,
there must be peace in the nations.
If there is to be peace in the nations,
there must be peace in the cities.
If there is to be peace in the cities,
there must be peace between neighbors.
If there is to be peace between neighbors,
there must be peace in the home.
If there is to be peace in the home,
there must be peace in the heart.
Lao Tzu

Lao Tzu says it powerfully but it's shorter and more powerful in reverse:

If there is to be peace in the heart,
we must create peace in the home.
If there is to be peace in the home,
we must create peace between neighbors.
If there is to be peace between neighbors,
we must create peace in the neighborhoods.
If there is to be peace in the neighborhoods,
there is no need for nations,
and there will be peace in the world.

Notes

1 Tamez, E. (1987), *Against Machismo*, Illinois: Meyer Stone, p. 14.

2 Girard, R. (2001), *I See Satan Fall Like Lightning*, New York: Orbis, p. 96.

3 Patel, R. (2009), *The Value of Nothing: How to Reshape Market Society and Redefine Democracy*, London: Portobello, pp. 42–43.

4 Patel, R. (2009), *The Value of Nothing: How to Reshape Market Society and Redefine Democracy*, London: Portobello, p. 166.

5 Sharp, G. (2010), *From Dictatorship to Democracy: A Conceptual Framework for Liberation* (4th edn), Boston: Albert Einstein Institution, p. 17.

6 Sharp, G. (2010), *From Dictatorship to Democracy: A Conceptual Framework for Liberation* (4th edn), Boston: Albert Einstein Institution, p. 18.

7 Tolstoy, L. (2006), *The Kingdom of God Is Within You*, New York: Dover, p. 21.

8 Andrews, D. (2008), *Plan Be: Be the Change You Want to See in the World*, Milton Keynes: Authentic Media, p. 5.

9 Rosenberg, M. (2003), *Nonviolent Communication: A Language of Life* (2nd edn), California: PuddleDancer.

10 http://www.citizensuk.org

11 Hopkins, R. (2008), *The Transition Handbook: From Oil Dependency to Local Resilience*, Totnes: Green Books. Or http://www.transitionnetwork.org.

12 http://www.ekklesia.co.uk/about/values

13 Prasad, D. M. C. (2007), *Lamenting Loss and Resisting Oppression: Towards Dalit Solidarity in Challenging Caste Oppression through Collective Laments*, Bangalore: ATC, p. 147.

14 Semelin, J. (1993), *Unarmed Against Hitler: Civilian Resistance in Europe, 1939–1943*, London: Praeger, p. 66.

15 Gaston, R. (2009), *A Heart Broken Open: Radical Faith in an Age of Fear*, Glasgow: Wild Goose, p. 52.

16 Wink, W. (2000), *The Powers That Be: Theology for a New Millennium, London*: Doubleday, p. 93.

17 Wink, W. (2000), *The Powers That Be: Theology for a New Millennium,* London: Doubleday, p. 57.

Circle Books

Circle is a symbol of infinity and unity. It's part of a growing list of imprints, including o-books.net and zero-books.net.

Circle Books aims to publish books in Christian spirituality that are fresh, accessible, and stimulating.

Our books are available in all good English language bookstores worldwide. If you can't find the book on the shelves, then ask your bookstore to order it for you, quoting the ISBN and title. Or, you can order online—all major online retail sites carry our titles.

To see our list of titles, please view www.Circle-Books.com, growing by 80 titles per year.

Authors can learn more about our proposal process by going to our website and clicking on Your Company > Submissions.

We define Christian spirituality as the relationship between the self and its sense of the transcendent or sacred, which issues in literary and artistic expression, community, social activism, and practices. A wide range of disciplines within the field of religious studies can be called upon, including history, narrative studies, philosophy, theology, sociology, and psychology. Interfaith in approach, Circle Books fosters creative dialogue with non-Christian traditions.

And tune into MySpiritRadio.com for our book review radio show, hosted by June-Elleni Laine, where you can listen to authors discussing their books.

MySpiritRadio